Nov. 2019

Memories of a Forgotten Place

Dennis L. Brewer

WESTBOW
PRESS®
A DIVISION OF THOMAS NELSON
& ZONDERVAN

This book is a work of non-fiction. Unless otherwise noted, the author and the publisher
make no explicit guarantees as to the accuracy of the information contained in this book
and in some cases, names of people and places have been altered to protect their privacy.

WestBow Press books may be ordered through booksellers or by contacting:

WestBow Press
A Division of Thomas Nelson & Zondervan
1663 Liberty Drive
Bloomington, IN 47403
www.westbowpress.com
1 (866) 928-1240

Because of the dynamic nature of the Internet, any web addresses or links contained in
this book may have changed since publication and may no longer be valid. The views
expressed in this work are solely those of the author and do not necessarily reflect the
views of the publisher, and the publisher hereby disclaims any responsibility for them.

Any people depicted in stock imagery provided by Getty Images are models,
and such images are being used for illustrative purposes only.
Certain stock imagery © Getty Images.

ISBN: 978-1-9736-7660-7 (sc)
ISBN: 978-1-9736-7661-4 (hc)
ISBN: 978-1-9736-7659-1 (e)

Library of Congress Control Number: 2019915607

Print information available on the last page.

WestBow Press rev. date: 10/17/2019

To My Grandchildren

Taryn Elanah Brewer
and
Walker Boaz Brewer

Contents

These Are Not My Hills

These are not my hills.
These rugged ancient sentinels of earth and stone,
armored with maple, walnut, oak, hickory, pine and spruce.
These are not my hills.
These are the hills of my father and his fathers before him.

These are not my hills.
These hills which cast dark, cooling shadows upon
nameless hollows and creeks that follow serpent's winding trail.
These are not my hills.
These are the hills of my mother and her mother's before her.

These are not my hills. These hills that cradle in their laps
rising spring fog and lingering summer mist.
These are not my hills.
These are the hills of my children and my children's children.

These are not my hills.
These brooding, nurturing hills joined hip to hip
as a sanctuary for animal and fowl in an endless march.
These are not my hills.
But I belong to them in thought and fleshly heart.

Prologue

In the preface of an earlier book, I had described it as *"a place unlike any other place"*. Those are the only words that might be used to describe it. Nestled in the quiet solitude of ancient hills, which time has forgotten, is a place of strength, hope, endurance and perseverance.

There are no factories or manufacturing concerns that call this place home. The natural topography of this place does not allow for major agricultural endeavors. There are no major highways or railways that traverse its terrain. There are no large cities that sprawl across its landscape.

The only claim to notoriety which this place holds is in the distinction of consistently being designated as one of the poorest counties in the nation. Yet, those who live in this place and those who hold memories of their years of growth in this place discovered that riches are not found in material possessions but in treasured relationships with family, neighbors and friends.

For some it might appear to be an insignificant and irrelevant place yet, for others it is the place of pleasant memories. For some it might seem devoid of accomplishment and the brunt of jokes yet, from its ancient womb there have been born and nurtured to adulthood doctors, lawyers, ministers, educators, politicians, and entrepreneurs of great accomplishment. From its creeks and hollows there has flowed a constant stream of mankind, each generation building upon the past and leading into the future.

This flow of native sons and daughters have touched society in all its spheres. Much like the quiet flow of countless branches with pleasant and descriptive names which pour from the hills and feed into Buck, Sturgeon, Island, Buffalo, Sextons, Wolfe and Indian Creeks to deposit their waters into the Kentucky River. This flow is not the end of their journey for the proud Kentucky then carries their precious cargo into the Ohio River that flows into the mighty Mississippi which empties into the endless Gulf of Mexico. In this manner have the lives, accomplishments and influence of the progeny of one place reached far beyond this *"place unlike any other place."*

For some, it is a place that can only be pointed to on a map and yet, in the words of John Green, *"The town was paper but the memories were not."*

It is a place that can never be recreated. It is a place that time can never diminish. It is a place of the past and present, the "was" and the "is" and that is what gives this place a uniqueness that no other can equal.

Enjoy these stories of this *"place unlike any other place"* and if you happened to grow to adulthood in this place, be thankful. If you did not, then attempt to visualize in your mind the pleasure you would have known had you had the opportunity to do so.

Dennis L. Brewer
Richmond, KY

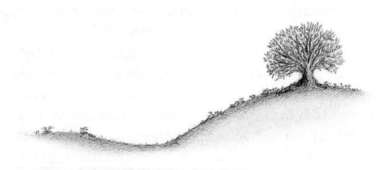

Chapter 1

Squirrels and Funerals

Saturday was my favorite day. Each Saturday morning I would usually climb out of bed, sneak downstairs into the living room and quietly turn on our television set. Stretching out on the couch I would await the arrival of my favorite cowboys. Soon they would ride through the air and arrive in my home, allowing me to share in their adventures and be amazed at their skill in fighting, shooting, and riding. As I would gaze at the test pattern on our small television, I couldn't help but wonder what exploits Roy, Gene, The Lone Ranger and Sky King would face on that morning!

Only one thing could prevent me from spending a few hours in front of the television on Saturday Morning. That one thing was an opportunity to go squirrel hunting with my friend, Jackie, and this was one of those Saturday Mornings.

I had slipped out of bed before day light and pulled on my clothes. I put a half-filled box of twenty-two cartridges into my pocket, picked up my flash light from the dresser, took my rifle from the corner of the room, and quietly made my way down the stairs and out the back door.

It was a cool morning in late October. The ground was covered with brightly painted leaves and everything around me seemed at peace. I turned on my flashlight and began my half mile journey to the home of Jackie Dooley. I would turn my flashlight off and then turn it back on again, moving the light in a circular and zig-zag motion as though I were playing with a sparkler on the fourth of July.

As I neared the half-way point of my walk on the narrow dirt road that led to Jackie's home, my thoughts of hunting were interrupted by a groaning sound. I stopped in my tracks, turned off my flashlight and listened. I heard the sound once again and it seemed to be ahead of me and off to the right. I turned the light back on and moved slowly toward the sound. The dim glow of the light revealed a pair of feet and then a pair of legs. As the light gradually sliced through the darkness, it continued its journey of revelation to bring to light an upper body with hands and arms and shoulders. Finally, the light came to rest on the face of Buford Thomas. His eyes were closed and he was moaning, "Please don't hurt me. Please, don't hurt me." I stood quietly for a moment, turned off the light and then, after hearing a little movement from Buford along with his trembling voice saying "Oh, dear God, help me!" turned it back on again. Once more, Buford, his eyes closed was jerking and trembling like mom's fresh wash hanging on the clothes' line during a windstorm. I smiled, turned the light off and then ran a few steps up the road. I stopped and turned to look back at the spot where Buford was lying. Once again, I could hear Buford moaning. Then I heard his footsteps as he ran down the dirt road away from me. It sounded like a galloping mule that had been scared by a rabbit.

I laughed to myself and thought, "What's wrong with that old man?" as I continued my pilgrimage to Jackie's home.

When I reached the foot of the hill below Jackie's home, I saw the yellowish glow of a flashlight on the front porch. It would blink on and off. I stopped and also blinked my flashlight and then, keeping the light turned on raced up the hill to the porch. The light finally revealed Jackie sitting on the edge of the porch with his twenty-two rifle laying beside him.

"Are you ready to bag us a mess of squirrels?" Jackie asked.

"I'm ready." I answered.

"I know just the spot. I've been listening to them the last couple of days and there is hundreds of them. We'll get into place just about daylight and be waiting for them." Jackie said.

Together we walked into the woods behind Jackie's home. Finding a place at the trunk base of a large Maple, we sat down to await the arrival of morning and the frisky squirrels as they jumped from limb to limb like acrobats on a circus trapeze.

As the dim light of a new day began to reveal our surroundings, I saw several large oak and hickory trees around us. I reached into my pant pocket and pulled out a plug of chewing tobacco, took a bite from the plug, and then handed it to Jackie. He took a bite, and with a smile handed the tobacco back to me. "Don't get no better than this." Jackie whispered. I nodded my head in agreement.

As the morning passed, we were able to kill five squirrels each before making our way back to Jackie's home. "Want to do something else?" Jackie asked.

"Nope." I answered. "I gotta get back home and go to a funeral with Daddy."

"Who died?" Jackie asked.

"Old Bill Callahan." I replied.

"You don't say!" Jackie exclaimed. "Old Bill from Booneville? The old black man that's always wandering around town and cleans up the Bank every day? I heard he carries a key to the Bank in his pocket."

"Yep." I responded. "Going to have his funeral today at the First Baptist Church and Daddy wants me to go with him."

"Sure wish I could go." Jackie said. "I liked that old man. He always smiled at me when I saw him. I guess he was about one of the best thought of men in the county."

"Funeral's at one o'clock." I said. "Why don't you come down to the house about noon and go with us? Daddy won't mind and there'll be room. Maybe after the funeral he'll let us go over to the novelty store and look at the new comic books."

"I'll be there!" Jackie said as he smiled.

On my way home, I thought about Old Bill. Only four black families lived in our county and they were all hard working, good people and thought of no different than any others. They attended our schools, ate where we ate and attended church where we attended. I remembered the first time I had met Old Bill. Daddy had taken me to town with him to do a few errands. We had gone to the restaurant on the town square for lunch.. Daddy had bought me a hamburger and

3

soft drink and we were sitting at a booth eating when Old Bill came in. He smiled at Daddy, walked over to our booth and sat down.

"Want something to eat, Bill?" Daddy asked.

"Might just eat some French fries and drink me a Coca-Cola." Bill told the waitress when she came to our table.

Soon she arrived with the order and as Old Bill began to eat, he and Daddy began to laugh and talk about the antics of some of the well-known politicians within the county. I couldn't help but stare at this old man whose skin was as black as soot. The only other people I had ever seen with skin that black were coal miners who would stop by the country store on their way home from work.

After the meal and on our way home I had asked Daddy if Bill worked in a coal mine. "No." Daddy had answered. "He farms and does odd jobs for people around town, cleans the Bank and a few of the barber shops. I don't ever know of him working in a coal mine."

I thought for a few minutes and then asked Daddy why Bill's skin was a different color than ours. Daddy had smiled and said, "Well, Dank, I guess God just loves different colors in His creation. Just look at the birds and butterflies. They're all different colors. Same way with grass and trees and the sky. God has a lot of different colors in this old world for us to enjoy and be thankful for. Shouldn't be any different with people, now, should it? He made some of His people white, some brown and others black and red and even yellow. Even gave some different shades of those colors, but inside, we're all the same. We think and feel. We laugh and cry. We even have the same kind of blood rushing through us. Don't ever forget this, Dank."

"I won't." I had promised.

I arrived at the back door of our home and saw Minnie Pearl, my aging beagle, laying quietly with her head resting between her outstretched paws. She raised her head and stared at me as I spoke to her and I held up the five squirrels. "See what you get for being such a sleepy head?" I asked. Minnie Pearl stood, tilted her head and stared at me. I laughed, patted her on the head and entered the house. I walked into the kitchen where Mom and Dad were sitting at the kitchen table, Dad was sipping a cup of coffee and Momma was peeling potatoes.

"Have any luck?" Dad asked.

I held the five squirrels up for him to see. Dad smiled and then said, "Come on and I'll help you clean them."

We walked back outside, and Dad took his sharp pocket knife from his pocket and we began to clean the squirrels.

"Jackie wants to go the funeral with us." I said.

"That's fine with me. We got plenty of room for his scrawny little body." Dad said with a laugh.

At noon, Jackie Dooley arrived, dressed in his Sunday best and we made the trip to Booneville. As we sped by the houses of our neighbors and familiar landmarks, Dad would speak jokingly to Jackie and me, kidding us about girls we knew and mischief that we had been involved in. He then asked, "Did either of you boys see anything out of the ordinary this morning when you went hunting?"

Both of us answered, "No" and then Daddy continued.

"Well, just wondering. I went down to the store this morning to get some gas for the truck and they were telling me about Buford Thomas getting a real scare this morning. I guess, from the way I understand it, he was coming out of the holler where you live Jackie and had a run in with some of those space aliens that was all over the news last month. You remember, that couple up north somewhere that got abducted by those space people."

"What did he say?" I asked.

"Well, I didn't speak to Buford but Conley told me what Buford told him. Seems he was coming out of the holler and saw this real bright light coming right at him. He slipped over to the side of the road and laid down so that maybe whatever it was wouldn't see him. Then he said he saw that light getting closer and closer and that it touched him right on his feet and started to move up his body. He said that light made him go blind as a bat and he couldn't see nothing at all. He didn't even know how long them space people stood there and looked at him but said he could feel their beady little eyes examining every inch of his body. Buford said the next thing he knew they had let him go and he didn't waste any time getting out of that holler. Conley told me that Buford warned everybody to be on the look-out and to keep their guns handy. Never know where they might show up next."

I smiled and then asked, "What did them space people look like?"

"Don't know. Like I said, Buford went blind from that paralyzing light they shined on him." Daddy answered. "He kind of suspects they was a scouting party from some UFO that was just looking around to find someone to take with them back to wherever they are from."

"Really?" I said.

"Yep." Daddy answered, "But you know what I think. Buford ain't got nothing to worry about. I believe they can find a whole lot better looking specimens than him if they have a lick of sense about them."

"I kind of wish them space people would come to my house," Jackie said. "They could take my sister back with them to wherever they're from. I don't think they would keep her very long though. If they did, we wouldn't never have to be worried about them anymore because she'd talk them to death."

We arrived in Booneville and Dad drove to the church parking lot. A large crowd of people had already begun to assemble for the funeral. After we parked the truck, Dad, Jackie and I made our way to the church, Dad would stop to speak or shake hands with other men along the way. As we entered the small church, it was evident that we would not be able to find a seat. I looked at those who were already seated and I was impressed by the large number of black people who were there. Men, women and children of all ages had made their way from Hazard, Whitesburg, Jenkins, Jackson and surrounding areas to this small town in order to pay their last respects to Old Bill.

"Here, boys!" Daddy said as he placed his hands on our shoulders and then pointed to a spot in the corner of the church. "You boys get over there in the corner and I'll stand over here. Just be quiet and don't do anything disrespectful now." Jackie and I nodded and made our way to the rear corner of the church.

Soon the undertakers arrived, pushing the large coffin down the aisle of the church followed by the family of Old Bill Callahan. As the coffin moved slowly toward the front of the church, I could hear the moans and sobs of those present along with an occasional outburst of wailing that I had not heard since Mavis Wilson's husband left her for another woman and I happened to be walking by her house right after he had left. Old Bill's family took their seats in the front pews of the church and after the coffin and flowers had been set into their proper place, the undertakers left and the Pastor of the church stepped behind the pulpit.

In a slow, monotone voice, he read the obituary, quoted scripture and then prayed. The choir, composed completely of white people, stood and began to sing in a slow, plodding manner "Amazing Grace, how sweet the sound, That saved a wretch like me.... I once was lost but now am found, Was blind, but now, I see...."

As the choir sang, I noticed two small black boys sitting in the pew a couple of rows in front of us. They looked at each other, raised their eyebrows and exchanged a look of disbelief at what they were hearing, and then bowed their heads and began to snicker. An elderly black lady, elegantly dressed and wearing a large hat leaned forward and with a quick motion, smacked each of the young boys in the back of the head and whispered, "You two hush right now. Them white folk are doing the best they can do." The two boys straightened their heads, sat erect and stared straight ahead.

After the choir had completed the last stanza and chorus of Amazing Grace, the pastor approached the pulpit. Brother Williams was an elderly man who was greatly loved by the members of the church and the entire community. He was a good man who had a style of preaching that was of a more dignified and teaching style than a foot stomping and pulpit slapping manner. He appeared grandfatherly as he stood behind the pulpit and took a moment to slowly examine each face in the congregation.

"There's only one reason we have come to this place this afternoon," he said "and that is to show our love and respect for Bill Callahan, one of God's precious children." Several within the congregation shouted, "Amen" or "Oh, yeeees."

Preacher Williams paused. I suppose he wasn't accustomed to having the congregation answer him in the course of his sermons. He then said, "Bill was a good man, a loving man....." and again voices answered, "Yeees, praise God!" and "Thank you Jesus."

After another pause Preacher Williams continued. "He was a loving husband" followed by an echo from the congregation of "Hallelujah! Yes, he was!"

Once more a pause and then Preacher Williams said, "A good loving father" followed with sobs and shouts of "Oh, Lord Yes.…. Yes, preach it brother" and "Praise God."

Then, something happened that I had never seen before. Brother Williams became transformed. It reminded me of Clark Kent, a mild-mannered news reporter suddenly being transformed into a man of steel. Pastor Williams began to preach with youthful vigor, discarding his carefully worded, slow and reserved voice for one that became filled with emotion. As he did, members of the congregation began to shout even louder encouraging him in the progress of the transformation. Soon, Pastor Williams, this grandfatherly figure entered into a rhythm as he moved from one side of the pulpit to the other side as if he were dodging some object that had been thrown in his direction while literally jitterbugging and becoming demonstrative with his hands and body as he would lean over to face the congregation, slap the pulpit with his hand, and then take an occasional stroll across the stage.

I studied the faces of the Choir seated behind the Preacher. Some stared at him with looks of disbelief while others grinned at each other with an occasional wink of the eye as they listened to his words and witnessed his antics.

All the while, the black members of the congregation continued shouting encouragement and Preacher Williams did not disappoint them. Jackie and I stared at each other and I noticed some of the men standing with us in the rear of the church smiling at each other and their stomachs vibrating with laughter that could not be released for the ear to hear.

Finally, the service came to a close. Preacher Williams took a neatly ironed white handkerchief from his pocket and wiped his forehead and then, with an air of pious dignity, stepped off the stage. The Choir behind him stood and began to sing "When we all get to heaven."

The funeral directors came forward and led by Preacher Williams, carefully rolled the casket containing the earthly remains of Bill Callahan to the foyer of the church. One of the Funeral Directors then returned and looking in the direction where Jackie and I stood, motioned for us to come to him. We did as he directed us and he whispered into my ear, "Dank, you boys can go on outside now."

As I walked through the foyer, I saw old Bill lying silent in the coffin, eyes closed, as though in a peaceful sleep. He was dressed in a white shirt, tie and blue suit and looked more dignified in death than he had ever looked in life. Jackie and I quickly left the foyer of the church, hopped down the front steps and took a place to the side of the building. We were followed by a steady stream of friends of Old Bill who had come to pay their last respects to a man they had each known and would certainly miss.

Small groups of men gathered and quickly lit cigarettes or placed chews of tobacco in their jaws. Women, dabbing their eyes with dainty white handkerchiefs and children stood together, carefully watching the others as they exited the church.

"Ain't never been to a funeral like this before," Jackie whispered to me. "Sure glad you asked me to come."

I nodded my head in agreement and whispered in reply, "This is about the best funeral I've ever gone to."

As we stood outside, I watched the steady flow of black people leaving the church. Two heavy set, elderly women came out with their arms locked together and with their free hands, wiping tears from their eyes and wailing with sorrow. Both were impeccably dressed and wore large fashionable hats tilted graciously on their heads. They made their way down the steps to a grassy area next to the church near where Jackie and I stood. One of the ladies, overtaken with the overpowering grief of the moment, slumped first to her knees, then sat back and finally fell onto the grass. She lay on her back, legs tightly together and her dress pulled modestly over her knees. Her companion knelt next to her and said, "Oh Sweet Jesus, she's fainted!" She then attempted to awaken her unconscious friend by gently shaking her body. When it became evident this gentle approach was not going to be successful, this elegant lady pulled back a small hand covered by a white glove and with the words "In the naaaaaaame of Jesus!" slapped her sleeping friend on the jaw. The sound reminded me of the sharp crack of my twenty-two rifle after I had just fired it.

This attempt to revive her friend was not successful and for a second time, she came back with her small hand, looked upward toward heaven and shouted loudly, "In the naaaaaaame of Jesus," slapping her friend with greater force and a louder crack than before. Jackie whispered to me, "If that woman don't wake up pretty soon that other woman is going to beat her to death."

One of the funeral directors appeared and, taking a small container from his jacket pocket, knelt next to the sleeping woman and placed it under her nose. She sat part way up, fell back and then sat quickly back up again. Looking around with surprise, she placed her hand on her jaw. The funeral director, along with her companion, took her short arms and lifted her to her feet. "I must have hit my jaw when I fell." She said to her companion.

"That's all right, Geneva. You'll be all right now." Her companion replied as she gently patted her on the shoulder.

I watched as the coffin was carried down the steep steps in front of the church. The men who stood by removed their hats and the women gently dabbed their eyes with their handkerchiefs as the coffin was placed in the long, black hearse and members of the family were settled into their cars and trucks. We stood silently until the hearse slowly pulled away from the curb and began its journey to Old Bill's final resting place.

Daddy came to where Jackie and I stood and said, "Boys, I have to go to the feed store and the hardware store. You two want to look around town for a little while and then I'll meet you in front of the court house in about thirty or forty minutes?"

"Sure." I answered. "We'll be over at Miss Campbell's looking at the comic books." Jackie and I turned and ran across the street, down the sidewalk and into the store. A bell rang as we entered the door and I saw Miss Minnie sitting behind the counter. "Well Dank, I haven't seen you in a while. What can I do for you young men?" she asked.

"We just want to look at your comic books." I replied.

"You go right ahead. Just got some new ones in this past week." She said smiling.

Jackie and I went to the rack and began to look over the new selection of comics...... Superman, Batman, Captain America, The Fantastic Four, Archie, Bugs Bunny, Tom and Jerry, and a treasury of other titles caught our attention. Jackie picked one off the rack and handed it to me. It was a Fantastic Four Comic Book showing hideous green creatures attacking the Fantastic Four. The comic book cover called them **"Skulls From Outer Space."**

"Recon this is what them space people looked like that Buford saw this morning?" Jackie asked. I looked at the comic book cover, shrugged my shoulders, handed it back to Jackie and then continued to look through the latest issue of Superman.

I heard the bell above the door ring and saw Betty Wilson come into the store. I had seen her at Old Bill's funeral earlier. Miss Minnie Smiled and greeted Betty cheerfully, "Well how pretty you look today, Betty." I saw Betty smile and straighten her shoulders. I wondered if Miss Minnie was looking at the same person I was seeing. Betty was probably one of the ugliest women in the county. I had heard some people say the only reason she managed to catch her husband was because he had to court her at night and didn't have a lantern to take courting with him.

"You been to Bill's funeral?" Miss Minnie asked.

"Yes." Betty answered. "One of the saddest things I ever saw in my life."

"Poor Old Bill will be missed for sure." Miss Minnie said.

"Oh, I'm not talking about that. I'm talking about the disgraceful spectacle Preacher Williams made of himself. I have never seen such cavorting and unholy actions from behind the pulpit by a preacher of the gospel in all my life."

Miss Minnie was one of those people who never talked about others and always gave everyone the benefit of the doubt, even when their actions may have been questionable. She quickly turned the subject to another topic. "Well I heard something this morning that has gotten me concerned."

Betty walked quickly to the counter and leaned over it, thinking perhaps she was going to learn some new piece of gossip. "What is it?" she whispered.

In the same tone of voice as earlier, Miss Minnie said, "Well I heard some of them outer space people have been right here in our county. Out at Vincent early this morning some poor man had a run in with them. People who have told me about it say that he was awful fortunate to get away from them with his life and all his body organs intact."

I looked up from the comic book I was reading to see Jackie staring at me.

"Oh, I've heard about that." Betty said. "They were talking about it over at the church before the funeral started. Mildred Morris told me that Buford Thomas was confronted by some little green creatures early this morning. I think there was five or six of them little devils, just like the ones who captured that poor couple up in New Hampshire last month. From what I hear they pretty much paralyzed Buford with some kind of gun that shot out a stream of light. Made him go totally blind for a little while. Then them space devils took him up to their spaceship and did unspeakable things to that poor man. After they finished prodding and poking on him, they brought him right back to the same spot they found him. Poor Buford didn't know how long they kept him in that spaceship but when they brought him back, not one minute of time had passed away. Then they just left him laying at the side of the road and went on their way. Probably to find someone else to torment or take away in their spaceship."

"Oh, my goodness!" Miss Minnie said, "I wonder if the Sheriff has been out there yet to talk to Buford."

"Hah!" Betty responded, "You mean that sorry, good for nothing Martin? He's the poorest excuse for protection that decent folk in this county could ever have. He's probably over there hiding under his desk right now."

"Dank, it's time for us to meet your Daddy." Jackie said.

I looked at the clock hanging on the wall behind Miss Minnie and

Jackie and I walked to the door to leave." You boys come back when you have more time" Miss Minnie called cheerfully.

"Yes Mam," Jackie and I said in unison as we left the store and raced to the front of the courthouse.

Daddy was already there, waiting for us and talking with some men who were sitting on what they called "The Liar's Bench." As we approached, I heard the name of Buford mentioned and the men were laughing. Daddy saw us and smiling said, "Well, there you are boys. Are you ready to go home?" We nodded our heads and walked together to the pick-up truck, climbed in and began the six mile trip back to our home.

As we drove, Daddy turned the radio on and I heard Patsy Cline singing, *"I fall to pieces, Each time I see you again, I fall to pieces, How can I be just your friend?"* The cool October breeze came through the half open windows of the truck and played mischievously in my hair. I looked at Jackie, who was sitting next to the door. The wind was also blowing his hair and like invisible fingers, caused his hair to twist, turn and sway in time to the sound of the truck engine like dancers on a dance floor. Unaware of his hair's antics, Jackie was staring intently at each house we passed along the way. "Been a real full day" I thought to myself. "Went all the way from Squirrels to a Funeral. Don't get much fuller than that."

Chapter 2

A Premonition

I was awakened by a loud clash of thunder unlike any I had ever heard before. It was a loud, rumbling that seemed to grow and grow until it caused the windows to rattle and then continued to roar for some time before finally whimpering and growing silent. I then heard rain on the tin roof above my bedroom. The watery fingers of heaven began to beat out a melody on the tin, slowly at first, each drop playing a single note, and then was joined by countless other watery fingers combining their single notes into a pleasant harmony of refreshing peace.

I slipped out of bed, closed the window in the bedroom and then lay back down. The sun had not yet announced a new day and as I drifted back to sleep, I had a strange premonition that something unusual was going to happen today.

As the first rays of sunlight entered my room, I opened my eyes once more. The sound of familiar activity from the kitchen downstairs reached my ears. I heard the voices of mom and dad. The aroma of country ham wafted up the stairs into my room, finding its way to my nose bringing a smile to my face and a low sounding rumble to my stomach.

I slipped out of bed, pulled on my blue jeans and t-shirt and made my way down the narrow stairs from my room into the kitchen. Dad was sitting at the table, drinking his breakfast coffee as mom placed the ham, biscuits, gravy and fried eggs onto the kitchen table. A small radio, setting on the refrigerator, played the newest Ferlin Husky song, "Since you've gone, the moon, the sun, the stars in the sky know the reason why I cry, Love divine once was mine, now you're gone."

"This rain is supposed to stop pretty soon," Daddy said. "I'm going to finish the bathroom job at the Baker's today and will probably eat in town. What's your plans for today, Dank?"

"Nothing much. Thought I would go up to Earl's house and maybe go fishing. There's a big ol' catfish in their pond that I would sure like to catch. Been in there for a long time and always seems to get off the line whenever it gets hooked."

"Well, a good mess of catfish for supper would be awful good." Daddy said, smiling as he filled his plate with eggs, biscuits, gravy and a slice of country ham.

"Just as long as the one who catches it, cleans it." Momma added and then continued, "Oh, and while I think of it, before you go running off somewhere Dank, I need you to run down to the store for me and get me a can of baking soda. All the family is coming down from Ohio and I got a lot of baking to get done today. We're all going up to your Grandma's this weekend."

Mom had six sisters. Four of them lived in Ohio and they would always make an end of summer trip down to my grandmother's home. While the grownups would talk and sing, my cousins and I would spend the day exploring in the woods, wrestling, or swimming in the creek.

"Sure, I'll go just as soon as I finish eating." I said.

"And don't you get down there and start listening to them old loafers telling their big tales and forget what I sent you for." Momma warned.

"I won't forget." I answered.

At some point, while we were eating breakfast, the rain had stopped. It had gone unnoticed because of our morning conversations and eating our breakfast. Following the meal and as the first streams of light began to filter through the kitchen window, Dad said, "Well, it seems to have stopped raining already. Guess I better get the milking done and the cow turned out into the pasture. Dank, you need to take the slop bucket and feed the hogs for me this morning. Be sure you mix in some of the hog feed from the sack."

"I'll run upstairs and get my sneakers," I answered.

After pulling on my sneakers, I grabbed the slop bucket from the kitchen and made my way to the feed shed. I mixed a good portion of hog feed into the bucket filled with leftovers from family meals and then took the bucket to the hog lot. The two hogs began grunting and brushing against each other as they rushed to the feed trough. Slowly I poured the bucket full of slop into the trough and then watched as the hogs nudged against each other and ate the mixture.

As I made my way back to the house, I noticed the sun had risen above the mountains that surrounded our home.

"Summer has sure gone by awful fast." I thought to myself. Only two weeks remained of summer vacation and then I would be entering the fourth grade at Needmore Elementary School. I had often wondered how the school had gotten its name. One of our neighbors told me it was because of the old country store located in the community. People would need more salt or need more sugar or need more of some other item and make a trip to the store to purchase it. My mother's cousin, who lived across the road from our home once told me it was because the people in the community always need more money.

I entered the house and started upstairs as momma said, "Dank, take the egg basket and gather the eggs for me this morning. I'm gonna need them all for my baking today. Be sure you check the hen house good."

I took the basket and made my way to the small chicken house. This was one place I didn't like to go. The smell was always terrible and you had to always wipe your shoes after leaving the small building. I entered the building and quickly collected eggs from the empty nests. Three of the chickens were still sitting in their nests and I carefully placed my hand under each one, collecting the eggs they were attempting to hatch into baby chicks. One of the old hens put up a real fuss and our old rooster came to the door of the chicken house to see what was causing all the commotion. I didn't like that old rooster and he didn't like me. He had long spurs on the back of his thin legs and quickly I walked to the door, shooed him away, and returned to the house.

"Now Dank," Momma said as I placed the egg basket on the table, "Get on down to the store and get my baking soda for me. Be sure you get the largest box of Arm and Hammer he's got... no make that two and then you get right on back home. Young man, you remember what I told you. Don't you get down there and start listening to those foolish old tales them men are telling and forget why I'm sending you down there to begin with."

"Ohhhh... I won't Momma," I said as I left the house.

Minnie Pearl, my aging Beagle Hound, peeped her head from the door of her doghouse and looked at me.

"Come on, Girl!" I commanded, "We got to get down to the store." She quickly came to my side and began to walk with me to the gravel road that ran in front of our home.

The sun had risen higher in the morning sky and as the rays of sunlight heated the earth, moisture from the rain the night before began to drift upward like steam from a boiling kettle of water. It was a thick hazy mist that seemed content to go no farther than the tops of the trees that lined the road.

We hadn't walked very far until Minnie Pearl stopped and growled. I also stopped and looked at her. She was looking farther down the road ahead of us and I couldn't see what had attracted her attention.

"Come on Girl," I said. "I don't see nothing, and we've got to hurry or Momma will be madder than a wet hen."

I began to walk again and Minnie walked with me still growling. Her gaze was always ahead of us.

We had walked only a short distance when I saw what was causing Minnie to snarl. It was a lone figure, seemingly crumpled at the side of the road."

"Now who in the world could that be?" I thought as we slowly approached the mysterious form.

Only as we came closer could I see that it was a man with his back turned to us and he appeared to be kneeling. He wore a checked flannel long sleeve shirt and overalls. He had a cap setting sideways on his head and I could hear him moaning and mumbling to himself.

As I came to where the man knelt, I walked around to face him and recognized who he was. His name was George Washington Mayes. He lived all alone not very far from our home. Many people in his family called him G. W., but all the people in the community called him Wash.

"Wash" I said, "Are you all right? What's wrong?"

Wash raised his head from his chest and stared at me, "No I ain't all right, Dank. I ain't all right none at all. I'm about the most useless thing the Good God ever placed on this earth. I ain't brought nothing but hurt to everyone I know. I ain't nothing but a carousing, moonshine drinking, card gambling piece of flesh that ought to be put out of his misery."

"Oh, come on Wash." I said soothingly as I placed my hand on his shoulder. "You ain't that bad. We all got our bad faults, but we can always be better."

"No Dank," I ain't never going to be no better. I was just sitting here thinking about my poor old Momma and Daddy. I sent them poor people to an early grave because of my riotous and reckless living. I was about the most wicked son any couple could have ever had."

"Wash, I thought your Momma and Daddy were both up in their eighties when they went to Heaven." I said.

"I know Dank, but they would probably have lived to be over a hundred if it hadn't been for me. And then there is my dear, sweet wife, Mable. She left me last year because of my drinking and cussing and carousing ways. She went all the way to Dayton, Ohio to get away from me. I don't blame her one bit. I'm just a useless pile of flesh and bones and ain't worth nothing to nobody."

"Come on Wash!" I scolded. "That ain't true. God loves you. He loves you a lot, Wash. You just need to ask God to forgive you of your sinful ways. It'll make a difference, I promise."

Wash stared up into my eyes. I saw the dirt on his face and the light streaks where tears had marked a trail across his rugged, leathery skin.

"Pray for me, Dank," Wash said. "You are one of the best boys in this whole community. I know you go to church and some folk say you might be a preacher one day. Pray for me, Dank... Please pray for me."

"I will Wash." I said. "I'll pray for you. I gotta to go right now. I got to get on down to the store and get back home or Momma will have my hide. But I'll be praying for you."

I turned and started to leave when Wash grabbed me around the legs. I heard Minnie Pearl snarl. "Hush Minnie," I said, "Wash, let me go.... I got to get on down to the store."

"No," Wash said. "I ain't going to let you go until you pray for me. Your Momma is a fine Christian lady, Dank, and I know she would understand and wouldn't begrudge one little bit having you to take a little time to pray for me."

"All right, Wash." I said. "Bow your head and close your eyes." I commanded.

I placed my hand on Wash's head, closed my eyes and prayed.

"Good morning, God. It's me and Wash standing here before you. I don't need a single thing God but Wash is in terrible shape. He needs your help in a terrible way, God. I'm asking that you just touch him and let him know that you love him. I know he ain't nothing but a wicked old sinner. I know he ain't nothing but a carouser and womanizer and drunkard, but just get hold of his old stone heart that's as black as the coal in these hills and squeeze it real hard to make him mend his ways. He might not look like much and he might be a sneaky old rogue of a scoundrel who would steal the hams right out of his neighbors smoke house, but you made him God and you can turn him into a gentle, loving and upright man. Do that God, I'm asking real hard, in Jesus's name.

After I finished the prayer I said, "There now, Wash. I've prayed for you. Let me go now so I can get on down to the store."

I saw a smile on Wash's face as he looked up at me and said, "Oh, thank you Dank.... Thank you... Thank you... Thank you.... I feel like a different man."

Wash let go of his grip around my legs and stood, wiping the mud off the knees of his overalls. "I'm going to walk down to the store with you, Dank." He said.

"Fine with me" I said as I turned to continue my journey to the store. Wash walked beside me and Minnie Pearl trotted ahead of us.

After a few steps, Wash said, "Dank, when you prayed for me, you said something about me being an old scoundrel that would steal hams out of a neighbor's smoke house.... Does your Daddy know I stole one of them hams out of your smokehouse?"

"Yep," I answered.

"I'm right sorry about that Dank. I was on my way home the other night and when I got in front of your house a terrible rain storm came up. It was awful late and I thought I would just get into your smokehouse to stay dry until the storm passed. Guess I had been drinking some and dozed off for a little while. When I woke up and made out all them hams hanging above my head, I thought about how good one of them would taste all fried up, so I give in to the temptation and took it. How in the world did your Daddy know it was me?"

"He found your cap. Guess when you dozed off it fell off your head and you left it in the smokehouse. Everybody's seen you wear that hat for years."

"Hmmmm." Wash said. "Is your daddy real mad at me?"

"Nah. When he told Momma about it he just said that you probably needed that old ham a lot more than we did and then laughed."

Wash and I entered the small store and Minnie Pearl curled up next to the door. When we stepped inside, I saw Gentry Green and Floyd Marcum sitting on a bench where they usually sat pretty much every day.

"Well, look what the wind just blowed in." Gentry said as he took a long puff on his thin stemmed Dr. Grabow pipe.

And then speaking to Wash said, "Good gracious, Wash. What happened to you? You look like you just been rode hard and put up wet." Gentry laughed and stomped his foot onto the hardwood floor.

"Don't know that it's any of your business, Gentry." Wash answered.

I walked to the counter where Conley, the owner of the store stood, and said, "Momma needs two of the largest Arm and Hammer Baking Soda you got and Daddy needs a plug of Apple chewing tobacco."

Conley retrieved the baking soda and chewing tobacco and placed them on the counter. "Let's see now" he said. That'll be forty cents for the baking soda and ten cents for the chewing tobacco, Dank."

"Just put the baking soda on our bill and I'll pay you for the chewing tobacco." I said.

Conley looked at me and grinned as I placed two nickels onto the counter. He shook his head as he placed the coins into the cash box. He then looked toward Gentry and Floyd and winked.

"You want me to put them all into a paper poke, Dank?" Conley asked.

"Just the baking soda." I answered as I took the chewing tobacco from the counter and placed it into my hip pocket.

Conley placed the baking soda into a paper poke and I turned to leave the store.

"Don't go running off just yet, Dank!" Gentry said. "Come on over here and talk with us for a little while."

"Ain't got time. Momma needs the baking soda and she done give me orders not to waste my time listening to all them foolish tales you fellows tell." I answered.

Floyd laughed and slapped his leg with a gnarled right hand. "I must say Dank, you got one smart momma."

"Wait up Dank." Wash said. "I'm gonna walk back up the road with you."

Wash followed me out of the store. Minnie Pearl stood to her feet and led us as we walked back up the road.

We didn't speak anymore until we came to the front of my home. "Got to go, Wash. See you later." I said.

"See you Dank. Thanks for making me feel better. I think I might just go to The Vincent Church this Sunday and get me a little taste of religion." Wash answered.

"That would be good Wash... Real good!" I said as I raced up the graveled drive to the house.

I entered the house through the back door and walked into the kitchen. Momma was standing at the stove with her back to me and was singing along with the radio. I heard a duet that included my mother and Patsy Cline as they sang, *I stop to see a weeping willow,*

Crying on his pillow, Maybe he's crying for me, And as the skies turn gloomy, Night winds whisper to me, I'm lonesome as I can be....

I set the paper poke containing the baking soda onto the kitchen table and said. "Got your baking soda, Momma."

Momma turned and walked to the table and opened the bag. "This will do just fine, Dank. Took you a little longer than I thought it would though. You didn't dilly-dally along the way to the store, did you?" She asked.

"Met Wash Green on the way and he was in terrible shape. He made me pray for him and told me he was going to church this Sunday." I responded.

"Lord have mercy! That would be a miracle." Momma said while Patsy sang in the background, "I stop to see a weeping willow, Crying on his pillow, Maybe he's crying for me, And as the skies turn gloomy, Night winds whisper to me I'm lonesome as I can be...."

"That man has been no good for as long as I have known him. He seems to get into more scrapes than any other ten men in this whole county." Momma added.

"I'm going to go on up to Earls now and do some fishing," I said as I turned to leave.

"You be careful Dank. Make sure someone is with you at that pond and don't you dare try to go swimming by yourself. No matter how hot it gets today and that's an order, young man!"

"All right Momma!" I yelled back as I left the house.

Minnie Pearl was lying next to the back door and just as soon as I stepped outside, she stood and gazed at me as if to ask, "Where we going now?" I smiled at her and walked to the warm house to retrieve my fishing rod and reel and fishing gear. I had dug worms the day before and picked up the can that held them in fresh moist dirt and began my walk to Earl Wilson's home. It was getting much hotter. This had been one of the hottest summers in the memory of many of the older people in the community and today's temperature was expected to go above a hundred degrees.

As Minnie Pearl and I walked beside the gravel road, cars and trucks would pass and blow their horns, waving at us as they went by.

Soon a truck stopped and Willis Morton asked, "Where you headed, Dank?"

"Up to Earl Wilson's house." I answered.

"Hop in the back. I'll give you a ride. Way too hot be walking on a day like this." Willis suggested.

I looked at Minnie Pearl and commanded, "You go on back home girl. I'll be back in a couple of hours."

I quickly climbed into the back of the pick-up. As the truck sped off, I saw Minnie staring at me and then she turned and trotted back toward home. I enjoyed the breeze against my sweaty skin as I rode the short distance in the back of the truck. Willis stopped in front of the Wilson's home and I climbed out. "Thanks!" I yelled and Willis waved at me as he sped off.

I walked to the back door of the Wilson's house and knocked on the screen door. I could see Myrtle, Earl's mother, in the kitchen. She came to the screen door and said, "Why Dank, what are you doing here?"

"Want to go fishing in the pond if it's all right?" I said.

"Why, mercy yes, Child. You know it's all right. You don't even need to ask. You go right ahead and fish all you want to."

"Would Earl want to go with me?" I asked.

"Well, I'm pretty sure he would if he was here but he went to help his dad over at his grandparent's home. They're doing some work on the tobacco barn I think. But if you are still here when they get back I'll tell him where you are."

Nodding, I turned and walked toward the pasture behind the Wilson's home. I set my fishing poles and can of worms through the pasture gate and then climbed over the gate. I took the plug of Apple chewing tobacco from my hip pocket, opened the wrapper, and then took a bite from the corner of the plug, allowing it to settle into my right cheek. I closed the wrapper back around the tobacco plug and placed it back into my pocket.

I walked another couple hundred feet to the edge of the three acre pond. As I looked at the pond I tried to determine the best place to sink my line. After picking what I thought to be the perfect spot,

I baited my hook, lengthened the line of my floater, and then threw the line out into the greenish blue water. Now it was just a matter of waiting.

As I sat on the bank of the pond I heard a flock of crows as they called at me from the woods above the pond. Dragon Flies skimmed across the smooth surface of the still water and a deer came to the edge of the woods and stared at me, curiously, perhaps to determine if I were a threat or not.

I tried to imagine what was happening beneath the surface of the water and I could just imagine that big ole catfish, that Earl and I had christened Ole Boy, swimming lazily across the muddy bottom of the pond in search of something to satisfy his empty stomach. I would gently pull the fishing line in hopes of drawing his attention to the baited hook.

After an hour I came to believe that maybe this wasn't a good day to fish after all and stood, getting ready to pull my baited line out of the water. Then, the floater darted beneath the surface of the pond and I grabbed the fishing pole, giving it a slight tug. I held the pole tightly and walked around the edge of the pond as the fish on the hook struggled to become free. For ten minutes or longer, we played a game of give and take. I would surrender a little bit of line and then slowly reel the line back in. "This is going to be a big one" I thought to myself. "You go right ahead Ole Boy, I got just as much time as you do"

After a few minutes longer, I began to slowly but steadily reel the fishing line back onto the reel. The floater reappeared and I could tell that the fish on the other end had just about surrendered. "Must not be Ole Boy," I thought to myself "or he would put up a bigger fight than this." A few more minutes passed as I slowly reeled in the line until the floater was laying on the bank of the pond. I walked to the edge of the water and picked up the floater and gently tugged on the fishing line. Then, I saw the biggest catfish I had ever seen in all my life as he came close to the edge of the pond just below the water. I was so surprised by the size of that thing I almost swallowed my chew of Apple.

I regained my composure and whispered, "Hello there big fellow. Now just how am I going to ever get you up here on this dry ground with me?" I didn't have a fishing net or anything else other than the rod and reel and the hook that the fish had in his mouth. I crept closer to the water and stared intently at the fish, pulling gently on the fishing line. I could tell that he had swallowed the hook and bait. "You must have really been hungry to swallow the whole thing," I said out loud, as though the fish could understand my words.

I heard a noise behind me and turned to see Earl approaching me. He waved and I motioned for him to hurry.

Earl came running to where I was kneeling next to the pond. "I think I caught him Earl." I said. Earl knelt beside me and also stared at the helpless fish. "That's Ole Boy, Dank.... That's Ole Boy you got on your hook."

"But how in the world are we going to get him out of the water? I'm afraid he might break my fishing line and I ain't got no net or hook or nothing."

"Daddy's got a big net at the house. I'll run home and get it." Earl said as he stood, turned, and ran back toward his house.

I continued to stare at the fish as I pulled him just slightly closer to the bank and nearer the surface of the water. I got as close as I could and continued to stare at him.

"Ole Boy" you sure look as if you've had a hard life," I whispered. His large mouth had been gashed and torn, probably from being ripped by so many fishing hooks in the past. As I stared into the large eyes of Ole Boy, I couldn't help but feel sorry for him. He was a proud fish and now he lay tired and helpless near the surface of the water gazing into the face of a young boy.

As I stared at the fish I began to think. For some reason I thought of Old Bud Bowman. Bud had a reserved seat on the bench at the country store before he died. I would sit and listen to Bud's slow, and sometimes faltering voice, as he spoke of his youthful days and the service he had provided our country in the army during World War I. He would talk about people who had long since passed from the stage of life and he would pause at times, his steel gray eyes reflecting a heart that was filled with sad emotion. His ever-present scraggly beard could not hide a face that had been worn and wrinkled by the hands of time. His long fingers had been distorted and scarred by arthritis, making it difficult for him to roll a cigarette or even hold a bottle of coca-cola, his favorite soft drink. For some strange reason, I equated Old Bud Bowman with Ole Boy.

"I can't keep this fish." I thought to myself as the crows talked with each other in the woods and the dragon flies hovered above the smooth water of the pond. "Don't seem right that a fish like this gets caught by a little boy like me. He deserves to be caught by an old man like Bud Bowman. Someone he can understand better than me and someone who can understand this old fish better than I can. Besides," I thought, "What fun would there be coming up here to fish without the challenge of catching Ole Boy."

I knew what I had to do. I reached into my pocket and pulled out my single blade Barlow knife. I heard the voice of Earl calling to me, "I got the net Dank! I got the net!" he shouted.

I didn't turn to acknowledge Earl and pretended that I didn't hear him screaming to me. I placed my hand with the opened knife into the warm pond water and slowly placed the blade as close to the mouth of Ole Boy as I could without frightening him. I then quickly cut the fishing line. Old Boy continued to just lay motionless, staring at me with his large black eyes. "Go on!" I whispered. "Go on! Get away from here!" Still he just lay peacefully, until I placed my hand onto his head and gave it a small tap. He twisted his body and then with a splash of water was gone back into the unseen depths of the bluish green and warm liquid of the pond.

Earl came to where I knelt at the edge of the water and knelt beside me. He had the fish net poised and ready to scoop up Ole Boy. "Where is he, Dank? Where's Ole Boy?" I held the end of the fishing line up for Earl to see. "Oh, Man!" Earl yelled. "That dumb old fish snapped the line! I believe that old rascal must have a little bit of the devil in him."

I sat silently as Earl threw the fishing net on the ground, stood and stomped his foot. He then said, "Well, I guess that if he got caught once, he can get caught again. Are you going to try and catch him again, Dank?"

"Maybe later.... Not today." I said as I stood, picked up my rod and reel and can of worms. Earl and I began our walk back to his house.

As we approached the pasture gate we saw Earl's father, Bruce coming toward us. We met at the gate and Bruce asked, "Well, where's Ole Boy. I want to get a close up look at that old fish. I've been trying to catch him for years."

"He snapped the line, Daddy!" Earl answered. After Earl spoke, I thought to myself. "Is it lying if you don't correct someone who jumped to a wrong conclusion and you know that they aren't telling something just the way it happened?"

"I had him to do the same thing to me once." Bruce said, interrupting my thoughts. "Well boys, there's always another day and you did something that I don't know of anyone else ever doing. You got an eye to eye look at that big ol catfish."

The three of us walked together back to the house. I talked with Earl for a short time and then began my walk back home. As I walked along the dusty gravel road, I looked up at the sky. The sun was beginning to make its daily trip behind the distant mountains and there was a reddish glow that seemed to reach with long narrow fingers into a blue sky, like a man hanging onto the edge of a cliff not wanting to fall.

I thought about the day. I thought of how pitiful Wash had looked that morning as he stared into my face and how tired Ole Boy had looked as he gazed at me with those large black eyes. Then I remembered my thoughts before all of this had happened. I remembered the thunder that had awakened me earlier that morning and my feeling that something different, something well out of the normal would happen that day. "I guess it has" I thought to myself and then was brought back into reality when Jason Moore stopped next to me in his old green pickup truck. "Hop in the back Dank!" he yelled, "I'll drop you off at your house."

Chapter 3

For God and Country

Luke Price was well known in our county although he pretty well kept to himself. He wasn't a hermit nor a recluse but he didn't mix a whole lot with people outside the community where he lived. I would see him at the country store from time to time and looked up to him as an honest, truthful and fearless man. When on rare occasions he came to the store, he would sit on the long bench near the warm morning heating stove and talk with the men who gathered there on a daily basis. He would listen attentively to their tall tales and laugh at their jokes, though I am certain he, like myself, had heard them dozens of times before.

One day after Luke had left the store, some of the men began to talk about him. From their conversations, I learned that Luke had served in the army during World War II and had distinguished himself in the Normandy invasion. He had been part of the 101st Airborne Division, the Screaming Eagles and I had seen the large tattoo on his right arm of an eagle and cross with the words, "For God and Country." He had also been in the battle of the Bulge and received a bronze and silver stars. I was amazed that he had also been recommended for the Congressional Medal of Honor and that because of some glitch in the paperwork it had not been awarded. He had even been offered a battlefield commission and refused it, preferring to remain part of the company and unit in which he served.

Gentry Gray said that Luke had also served for a time as a sniper.

From the time he was a small boy, Luke had been known for his skill with a rifle. He could drive a nail at fifty paces with a twenty-two rifle and had just as much skill with a nitro hunter shotgun, always winning the local turkey shoot at Thanksgiving.

Perhaps the reason I admired Luke so greatly was because my brother was serving in the army in Frankfurt, Germany at the time and, although Luke was much older than my brother there was a similarity between the two that made me feel good whenever Luke was around me. Both were over 6 feet and two inches tall and both had played basketball for the county high school. Both had black hair and piercing black eyes and walked with a manner that spoke of confidence and fearlessness.

From the conversation of the men, I also learned that Luke had left High School during his senior year and volunteered for the Army after Pearl Harbor. He had been a pretty good basketball player, so good in fact that Adolph Rupp had made a visit to watch one of his games during his junior season. He had even offered Luke a scholarship to the University. That had all been put on hold however, and Luke, thinking he would be fighting the Japanese, was assigned to the American forces in the European theatre.

Luke would not talk about the war or what he had experienced. When asked about it, he would just stare at the person or turn his head away as though he had not heard the question.

After returning home from the service, Luke married his childhood sweetheart and they bought a small farm on Neeley Branch. A child had been born to the couple, but the marriage did not last very long. Some of the men believed it was because of Luke's love for the bottle. He drank pretty heavily and most in the community were divided on whether he drank because he liked the taste of moonshine or because he just wanted to forget his war experience. Whatever the reason, Luke had returned home one day to find that his new wife and baby girl had left, leaving a note telling him not to try and find them. Evidently, he hadn't. He continued to live alone on the small farm, drawing a small pension for injuries received during the war and tending a small crop of tobacco as well as raising livestock.

Near Halloween on my ninth year, I had visited with Gentry and Nora Gray, who lived just across the narrow road from our home. As we sat in the shade of a large oak tree Gentry and I talked. Gentry had laid down on the cool earth in the small front yard. The arrival of Halloween was mentioned and Gentry asked what costume I was going to wear. I had not yet made my plans but Gentry laughed and then shared with me a story about Luke.

The year after Luke's wife and daughter had left him, three of the young boys in the community decided they would play a Halloween prank on Luke. Late in the night on Halloween the three boys had slipped up to Luke's home. They had taken a cigarette, broken it into two pieces and then lit each of the halves of the cigarette. They then placed the fuse of a cherry bomb into the unlit end of each piece and positioned them on each end of the porch of Luke's small house. They had then run and hidden behind Luke's old black pickup truck. Soon, one of the cherry bombs exploded. Lights appeared in the house and soon the porch light came on. Luke appeared on the porch, holding his old shotgun and dressed only in his boxer shorts and tee shirt. As he stood, looking in each direction, the second cherry bomb exploded. Luke had jumped from the porch and pointed the shotgun in the direction of the explosion. The three boys thought the sight to be hilarious and began to laugh hysterically. Luke had heard their laughter and walked to where they were hunkered down behind the truck. Within a period of two minutes, Luke had broken two arms and a leg between the three pranksters. He had also broken one jaw, two noses, and blackened four eyes. With the three young boys lying on the ground, moaning and groaning Luke had turned, gone back into his house, turned off the lights and went to bed.

The next day, the three boys appeared in the office of Dr. Ager to have their bruised, broken and mangled bodies repaired. When Doc heard what had happened, he had laughed and said, "I would have given anything to have seen that. The next time you boys decide to play a prank on Luke Price you come and get me first. It would have to be better than any picture show, and I won't charge a dime to bandage you boys up after it's all over." For month's afterward, the three boys were objects of humor throughout the entire county. The event also served to bolster Luke's reputation as being the most dangerous man in the county as well. A good many of the people hoped Luke would run for sheriff. He didn't.

The following March I had returned home from Needmore School and saw the cars and trucks of all my relatives setting in our driveway. As I approached the house, I could hear the sound of crying coming from inside. Immediately I thought of a dream I had dreamed the previous week. For three successive nights, I would awaken following a dream. In the dream, Johnny, would appear at the foot of my bed and awaken me. He would then tell me that our mother was going to die. I remember asking him how that was going to happen, and he would always point to the window and there would appear the picture of a heart. The dream would then end. I would always awaken in a sweat with my heart racing and have a restless sleep following the dream. As I raced toward the back door of our home, my heart moving much faster than my legs, my mind imagined that the dream had come true and when I entered the house I would be told that my mother had died.

As I raced through the back door, my Uncle Lee grabbed me, knelt in front of me and hugged me. "I've got some bad news, Dank." He said. "Momma, where's Momma?" I asked. "She's in the living room." he replied. "But Dank, I've got some bad news.....Your momma and daddy got a telegram today telling them that your brother Johnny is dead."

I pulled free and ran to the living room. I saw Momma sitting on the couch between two of her seven sisters. They had their arms around her shoulders and Momma was slumped over with her face buried between her hands sobbing. Her body was shaking uncontrollably, and I stood in front of her. My aunts looked at me, tears in their eyes and then Aunt Bessie said, "Dank's home Emma." Momma raised her head, stared at me and then drew me near to her with a firm yet loving grasp. I felt the warm wetness of her tears as they bathed my cheek. Nothing was said as Momma continued to sob and tremble. I had also wanted to cry but a promise from the past became a dam that would not let the tears release the stinging pain felt within my heart and soul. After sitting with Momma for a time, I stood and walked through the house, out the back door and to the barn. I sat down on a bale of hay. As I looked around me, the surroundings that was as familiar to me as my own thoughts, became a blurred and strange setting, real but unreal in my mind as unreal as the thought that my brother was dead. For some reason, I thought of the tattoo that Luke Price had on his arm. I wondered if Johnny had a tattoo. I said the words, "For God and Country." and then, gripped by a pain I had never felt before, said to myself, "We need Johnny more than God does and more than our country does."

The next day we received a notice from the Army telling us that the body of my brother would be shipped home and that it would arrive in ten days. For the next few days everything seemed to be a mist and I was merely drifting along in a daze, living in a world of reality but trapped in an emotional whirlwind that I had never experienced before. It was a time of knowing yet unbelieving that this could be happening to me and my family. Each room of our home that I entered reminded me of Johnny. The cuckoos of the cuckoo clock he had sent to us from Germany caused me to think of him. The rifle sitting in the corner of the kitchen reminded me of the hours we had spent hunting in the woods behind our home. When I fed the hogs each evening, I thought of the time we had built the hog pen and remembered the sweat dripping from his face as he dug the post holes. Each thought brought to me a new temptation to remove the promise dam and allow the tears to flood in a torrential stream down my cheeks. But a promise was a promise and it was the last promise I had made to Johnny.

Each time the temptation to cry presented itself, my mind would transport me to a moment in time which seemed as though it were only yesterday. Johnny had announced to the family one evening at supper that he had enlisted in the army and would not finish his senior year of High School. At first, I had thought it to be a personal distinction, one which I could brag about to my friends at school. My brother was in the army, a soldier in uniform, and I knew in my mind that he would become more famous than Sergeant York or Audi Murphy. It had been a matter of pride for me until the day arrived when Johnny was to report for training at Fort Knox. It had not dawned on my young mind that he would be leaving home and that he would no longer be there to offer me advice, wrestle in the front yard, hunt in the woods behind our home, or administer to the scrapes and bruises I seemed prone to experience. When it became real to me that Johnny was leaving, I had slipped out of the house and hidden in my favorite hiding place. In my young mind, I had reasoned that Johnny could not leave without first telling me good-bye and, if he could not find me to say those words, then he would have to remain, and things would be as they had always been. As I crouched in the corner of the smokehouse, I heard the door open and Johnny appeared. He walked toward me and kneeling in front of me held out a small tin pig that clanged with the change that it contained. "I gotta leave Dank, but I wanted you to take care of this for me until I get back home. Will you do that for me?" I shook my head from side to side, determined that I would not do anything that might hasten Johnny's departure. "Well, I can't take it with me and I have to leave, Dank. I made a promise to our government and we always have to keep our promises. I'll just set this little fellow down here and maybe you'll change your mind." Johnny set the piggy bank down on the plank floor in front of me and then reached out and patted me on the head before standing. As he turned to leave I jumped to my feet and ran to him, grabbing him around his legs and clinging to him tightly. I began to cry, sobbing gasps of anguish deeper than any I had ever known before releasing a torrent of tears to flow down my cheeks. Johnny stopped in his tracks, reached around to touch me and then turned to face me. Once more he knelt in front of me. "It's all right, Dank!" he said. "Why, I'll be home before you know it and I'll write to you every day." Then, taking a handkerchief from his pocket, he wiped my face and said, "Hush now, don't go crying on me. Soldier's don't ever.... they don't ever cry and you are a little soldier, Dank. Promise me now. You don't see me crying, do you? Promise me now you'll never cry and when you start to let them tears flow, remember your promise."

"But I don't want you to go." I sobbed. Johnny looked into my tear-filled eyes and said, "I know but this is something I have to do, Dank. It's something I've always dreamed of doing. I know you wouldn't want to begrudge me that, would you?" I shook my head "no" and then, looking into his piercing but kind eyes said, "I promise, Johnny. I promise. I won't cry anymore." Johnny smiled and once more hugged me and then stood to leave. I followed behind as he walked to the car that would be taking him to Fort Knox and waved as he went out of my sight. From that moment onward, each time there was a temptation to cry, I would refuse to allow the tears to appear in my eyes. Whether it was a scraped knee, bloody nose from a fight at school, painful disappointment. or the stinging words of ridicule from a friend, tears could not breach or overflow the dam of a promise that I had made to a brother I loved.

The day arrived for the body of my brother to be delivered to us. My father had made arrangements with the King Justice Funeral Home to pick up the body at the train station and transport it to our home. The Funeral Home would be in charge of all the arrangements, but the body would lay in state in the small living room of the home my brother had known as his own. It was in this room that we had gathered as family each evening, listening to the radio, sharing the events of the day, entertaining neighbors and family or just sitting quietly, basking in the love that was felt and confirmed by acts, though not always exposed by spoken words.

My Aunts, Uncles, and cousins had gathered at our home and were preparing for the arrival of my brother. I stood outside in our front yard, my eyes gazing intently at the sharp curve in the road some distance from our home. I saw the black hearse, followed by my father's pick-up truck and another car close behind him. All three vehicles pulled into our drive. I continued to watch closely as the funeral directors exited the hearse, Dad from his truck and a soldier, dressed sharply in his dress uniform emerged from the third vehicle. Uncles and Cousins appeared from the house and together they carried the silver colored coffin into the house and into the living room, placing it at a spot that had already been prepared for it. When the coffin lid was opened, I looked at the thin ashen face of my brother. It was not as I had remembered him. The black, piercing eyes were closed. The full smiling lips were replaced by thin straight lines. The jaws that had been full of the glow of life were sunken and pallid. It was at that moment I surrendered to the truth and accepted the reality that my brother was really dead.

The next few days were filled with activity. A constant stream of family and friends made their way to our home and joined with our family in our time of mourning. Each hour of the day was filled with conversations, forced laughter, crying, and necessary chores performed by routine which required no real thought. At times, I would walk into the woods behind our home, seeking a time alone to be absorbed in my thoughts and express my anger toward God and Country which had taken my brother from me. The oak and maple, walnut and hickory trees seemed to sense my anger as their limbs, swaying in the early spring breezes, seemed to whisper to me that it was only natural I feel anger and gave witness to my expression of that anger as I kicked the leaf covered earth beneath me, or shook a small clenched fist toward the sky above me. Those trees, each as familiar to me as my own body, quietly endured my onslaughts of anger as I thrashed their sturdy trunks with gnarled, fallen limbs.

On the day of the funeral we had followed in a procession to the two-story church I knew well. My Great Grandfather had been part of the organization of the church and served as its Clerk. From that time, my Grandfather, uncles and father had been part of the church as Deacons and other family members held prominent places of leadership. When we arrived, the church parking lot was filled with cars and people. As we made our way into the already filled church, I overheard one of the men say, "I ain't never seen this many people at a funeral before. This has got to be the biggest funeral ever held in this county." Three preachers, all friends of the family, each spoke, though I could not concentrate on what they said. Following the service, we traveled a short distance to the family cemetery. Six young soldiers carried the coffin containing the lifeless form of my brother up the steep hillside as we followed slowly behind. At the top of the hill, I saw the freshly dug open grave that had been prepared earlier, by relatives and other men within the community. I had thought to myself, "Johnny will like it here. He's close to Grandpa and Ralph (my brother who had died as a baby before my birth), and family. He's close to the woods that he loved." After we took our seats, I looked at the large crowd of people that filled the small cemetery. The men were holding their hats in their hands, women were wiping their eyes with small handkerchiefs, children were sitting on the grass, and then I noticed Luke Price. He stood off by himself, leaned against a large Walnut tree at the edge of the cemetery. He looked solemn and his eyes seemed to be looking beyond the open grave, coffin and even the people who were gathered there. He had the look of a man that had drifted into another world uninhabited by anyone except himself. One of the ministers spoke, occasionally pausing to regain his composure, followed by a bugler as he sounded the melancholy melody of Taps. Seven soldiers then followed the commands of their superior and presenting their arms fired three volleys each from their rifles. Following the grave side service, we began to make our way off the hillside and back to our cars. Little Wallace Hamilton came running to me and handed me six empty brass cartridges that had fallen to the ground when the soldiers presented their 21-gun salute to my brother. I smiled at Wallace and he nodded his head and then ran away. I placed the cartridges into my pocket.

After a week, things began to return to a more normal routine for our family. There were periods of time when mom would burst into tears, Dad would go wandering off by himself and always seemed to be lost in his thoughts whenever anyone spoke to him and I suppose that even I was constantly distracted, allowing myself to drift into thoughts of the past.

About a week after the funeral, I walked to the country store. I entered the store, walked to the pop cooler, drew out a Nehi orange soft drink and went to the counter. I placed a nickel onto the counter. Conley, the store owner, smiled at me and then pushed the nickel back toward me. "It's on me today, Dank." I smiled at Conley, retrieved my nickel and walked to the porch. I set a coca-cola pop case on its end and made a seat for myself. There old men were sitting on the long bench next to me, whittling, smoking and chewing. We sat in silence for a good period of time and I thought to myself, "I don't think I can ever remember these old men being quiet this long." Finally, Willie

Neeley spoke, "Sure am sorry about your brother, Dank. He was a good boy. Well thought of. Yes sir... He was a mighty fine boy."

George Moore reached a plug of Days Work chewing tobacco toward me and asked, "Want a chew, Dank?"

Frank Botner said, "No! He don't want no chew of that tobacco!" And then, reaching into the bib of his overalls pulled out a plug of Apple chewing tobacco, took a hen and rooster knife from his pocket, cut off a piece and handed it to me." "Dank chews Apple. You know that George. You can slip that into your jaw after you finish your pop, Dank." I took the tobacco from Frank and smiled.

The old men began to talk about crops already planted and crops they intended to plant when Luke Price pulled into the store parking lot and stopped at the gas pump. He got out of the truck and glanced in our direction as he walked to the pump and began to put gas into the truck. After filling the tank with gas, Luke walked into the store and soon returned to the porch. He looked at me and smiled. "Dank, I got a new baby calf down at my place and I want you to get a look at her. Want to ride down there with me and I'll bring you right back here." I stood and said, "Sure. I'd like to see her," and walked with Luke to the truck and climbed into the passenger's seat. As we started to pull from the store, I looked at the old men sitting on the bench. Their mouths were open and they were staring at each other. Like me, they had never known of anyone other than Luke sitting on the seat of this truck. He wouldn't even pick up hitchhikers or anyone else walking beside the road no matter how well he knew them, and any time you saw the old black truck, you would see only Luke sitting behind the steering wheel.

"Sorry about your brother, Dank." Luke said as we sped along. I had the window rolled down and the wind felt good against my skin as I gazed at the homes of people I knew well.

"I know." I answered. Neither of us spoke again until we turned off the main road and traveled about a half mile up a dirt and gravel lane that led into the parking lot of Luke's home.

"Well, this is it." Luke said as the truck slid to a stop. We both got out of the truck and Luke said, "I need to get something out of the house, Dank. You sit on the porch and wait for me."

I followed Luke to the house and sat on the edge of the porch. I had never been to Luke's home before. The small frame house needed a fresh coat of paint and a couple of the gray painted boards on the floor of the porch needed to be replaced, otherwise everything seemed to be pretty well in order.

Soon Luke reappeared on the porch, holding a bottle of Pabst Blue Ribbon beer in one hand and a coca-cola in the other. "Here Dank" he said as he handed me the bottle of coke. "Come on down to the barn with me and get a look at that new calf."

We walked the short distance to the large tobacco barn and entered the double doors. Luke led me to a small stall and then pointed, "There she is. Have you ever seen anything as pretty as that in all your life?" The calf had the fawn color of a deer and when she turned her head, I saw what appeared to be a white cross on her forehead between two large brown eyes.

"Why's she got that cross right in the middle of her eyes, Luke?" I had asked.

"That makes her special, Dank," He answered. "We ain't got many Catholics around here that I know of but when I was in the army, I saw a lot of catholic boys make the sign of the cross on their chest just before we went into battle. Guess they thought it would protect them or, maybe just let God know they were thinking of Him before they died." Luke paused for a moment and then continued. "Ain't that something? People will spend a lot of good money to buy a little gold cross to wear around their neck. Maybe to let people know they was thinking of Him in case they died. And here, God has already put a cross right in the middle of the head of that little dumb calf. Ain't that something?" he said shaking his head.

As we turned to leave the barn Luke asked me. "Did the army tell you how your brother died, Dank?"

"Yeah." I replied. "They said he was in a car wreck. Must have had a heart attack that caused him to crash his car into a big tree."

"Was he driving his own car?" Luke queried.

"I think so." I answered. "Said he was on duty and in his regular clothes, too."

Luke stopped and smiled and said, "Dank, you need to tell your Daddy to contact old John Sherman Cooper and ask him to find out how your brother died. Don't make sense to me that he would be in his civilian clothes, driving his own car and still be on duty. Seems to me there's something more to it. Your brother wrote to me a couple of times and I feel there's something more to this than meets the eye."

"I will, Luke." I said.

"Well, Dank, let's get you back down to the store. Just set your empty bottle there on the porch." I set the empty coke bottle on the porch and then climbed into the truck with Luke.

"Don't know if you ever knew or not Dank but your brother use to help me on the farm some. He was probably a couple of years older than you but he could do the work of a full grown man. He was always pestering me and wanting me to tell him about the army and what it was like to fight in battles. I guess I probably told your brother more about me and what I went through than any other living soul. I hoped it might persuade him not to get mixed up with the army. Don't look like it did though." Luke paused and I saw that same look in his eyes that he always had when some of the men at the store would ask him about his war experience. He then continued, "War ain't never like they try to show it in picture shows. War can turn a normal boy into an animal whose only aim is to stay alive. You do whatever you have to do and kill whoever you have to kill just to stay alive or to keep those who are close to you alive. Ol General Sherman once said that 'War is kinda like what you would find in hell.' Well, if it is, then I guess I've seen it first hand and right up close and lived in the middle of it. I know one thing, Dank. If the Hell in the Bible is worse than what I've already seen, then I shore don't want to spend all eternity there."

Luke pulled into the store parking lot and I slid out of the seat. He looked at me, smiled and then made a sharp turn onto the road and sped off toward his house.

I walked to the porch of the store, jumped up on it and let my legs dangle over the side. All of the old men had left and as I sat alone, I remembered the sliver of tobacco that Frank Botner had given me earlier. I placed it into my right jaw, hopped off the porch and walked home.

That night at supper I mentioned to Daddy what Luke Price had suggested. Daddy had looked at me and then Momma and said, "Emma, Luke Price knows more about things like this than any man I know. I'm going to write Cooper a letter tonight and mail it out first thing in the morning."

Two weeks later we received a letter from Senator Cooper informing us that Johnny had been assigned to military intelligence and had been serving in that assignment for the past year. He was definitely on duty, in civilian clothing, and in his personal vehicle at the time of his death. His death had occurred under suspicious circumstances, but the Senator was unable to divulge those circumstances or the reasons behind them.

June arrived and with-it summer vacation from school. I normally looked forward to the arrival of June but this one was different. It was a month that brought with it a sense of melancholy. June would have been the month Johnny would have completed his tour of duty in Germany and his enlistment in the Army would have ended. He would have been returning home for good.

The first week following the close of school for the summer, I left home about mid-morning and walked to the store. Several of the old men had taken their customary spots on the porch, sitting on benches, upturned pop cases, or the edge of the porch. I went into the store, bought a Nehi Orange pop and returned to the proch, sitting on the porch edge allowing my feet to hang over the side. Some of the men were deeply engrossed in a checker game being played by Will Moore and Gentry Gray. Bige Davis watched each move they made and occasionally would say "aaaaaah" and then grunt. Finally, Gentry said, "Bige, you sound just like an old Billie Goat. How do you expect a man to play a decent game of checkers with you making them dad-blamed noises?" Bige leaned back and said, "I ain't doin' no sich a thing." I suppose that if Bige had just placed a "bah" in front of the "aaaaah" he would have sounded like a Billie Goat. I looked at Bige and smiled, thinking to myself, with that little white goatee he has on his chin he kind of reminds me of a Billie Goat."

"Yes, you are, Bige." Will piped in. "Now hush up and let us finish this here game in peace."

David Green pulled into the store parking lot and slowly slid from the seat of his old Studebaker truck. He walked slowly to the porch, spoke a word of greeting and then took a seat next to me. "You fellers hear the news yet?"

"What news you talking about?" three of the men said in unison.

"They found Luke Price dead this morning." David said.

Gentry and Will stopped their game of checkers and looked at David. "Luke Price? What happened?" Bige asked. I felt an emptiness fill my stomach.

"Well, Mose Barker lives right next to Luke and he found one of Luke's cows that had gotten out of the pasture. He took her back home this morning and saw Luke's truck in the front yard and the door standing wide open. He put the cow back into the pasture and then commenced to look for Luke to tell him that he probably needed to walk his fence line and find out where the old cow had gotten out at. Couldn't find him nowhere so he got a little bit concerned and went into the house hollering for Luke. He found him in his bed, dead as a door nail."

"What killed him? Was he shot?"

"No. They found four empty quart mason jars right next to his bed. They all smelled like moonshine so they figured he had just drunk too much too fast and his heart just stopped on him."

I finished drinking my pop and started the walk back home. As I walked, I stopped to sit on the side of the road, overlooking a clear, flowing creek. I thought about Luke and I wondered what his last thoughts, if any, might have been. I wondered about where he was right now, heaven or hell. I hoped that it wasn't hell as I remembered his words to me earlier about war.

Daddy took me to the funeral home for the visitation. I saw a large flag draped over Luke's coffin. His eyes were closed and a slight smile had been placed on his thin lips. The next day, Daddy, Momma and I attended the funeral of Luke at the little Methodist church within the community. The Choir sang and the Methodist Preacher said a few brief words and then we followed with the small crowd as six soldiers carried the coffin to the adjacent cemetery. Luke would be buried next to his mother and father and a baby sister that had died when she was very young. Once more, I watched as seven soldiers stood solemnly and then fired three shots each from their rifles. I heard the bugler as he played Taps and then the crowd moved from the cemetery toward their cars. No one spoke and I saw the gleaming of tears as they slid down my father's sun bronzed cheeks. "He's remembering Johnny." I thought to myself.

About the second week of July, I was in the garden picking green beans for Momma. Two of her sisters were coming that day and were planning to help her can the green beans for use during the long winter months. I saw a pick-up truck with cattle racks pull into our barn lot. I stood and watched as Rhea Smith climbed from the truck and started toward our house. Rhea saw me standing in the garden and hollered at me. "Hey, Dank. Come on down here. Got something fer you."

I left the garden and walked to where Rhea stood at the side of his truck. "Brought you a calf, Dank." Where can we unload her? I looked between the rails of the cattle racks and saw the calf that Luke had taken me to see on his farm.

"Luke Price wanted you to have this calf, Dank. They found a note in his bureau saying the calf was yours. He had wrote down the address of his wife and girl so they could be notified if anything ever happened to him. Guess they'll be coming in before long to settle his affairs."

"Just back your truck over here and we can unload her, Rhea." I said.

We unloaded the calf and I led her to the barn and placed her into a stall. Rhea walked with me and as we returned to his truck, he stopped and said, "Oh, I almost forgot Dank. Luke wrote a letter to you. Here it is with your name on it." and he reached into his hip pocket and drew out a folded letter and handed it to me.

Rhea got into his truck and pulled away and I walked to the barn. I sat down on a bale of hay and opened the letter.

"*Dear Dank*

> *Hope you enjoy raising this calf. She's a good one all right and I think God made her just especially for you. You can name her whatever you want but I've been calling her Promise. That little cross on her forehead reminds me of the saying, "cross my heart and hope to die" whenever you make a special and firm promise to someone and sort of like God's promise of eternal life through the cross. You're a good boy, Dank and one day I know you'll make something special out of yourself. And whatever you do, believe that God loves you more than He loved His own self..*

Your friend,
Luke."

I folded the letter back up and stuck it into my pocket. Once more I felt the tears begin to form behind my eyes and once more, I allowed the mental dam to be constructed by a promise made to keep the tears stored within me. I bit my lower lip and in a moment's time there flashed through my thoughts the face of my brother and Luke, both smiling at me. In my thoughts I saw the flag draped caskets, heard the bugles rendition of Taps and the report of rifles echoing throughout the hillsides. I thought of the words, "For God and Country" and in an instant the tears appeared.... washing my cheeks with torrents of salty liquid drops and causing my small body to tremble as I sobbed uncontrollably. "I'm sorry Johnny!" I moaned between intakes of labored breaths "I'm sorry.... I don't want to be a soldier anyway."

Chapter 4

The Resurrection of Rooster Reynolds

Jackie Dooley and I walked, as we did each weekday morning, the narrow, winding gravel road to Nevermore School. We would each place a thin slice of chewing tobacco in our jaw, careful that there were no prying adult eyes to notice what we had done.

We would often interrupt our walk to peer into the small creek that ran beside the road, throw gravel at curious squirrels that raced effortless along the branches of oak and walnut trees that dotted the road side, or mimic the caw of crows that circled above us.

Only a few weeks of school remained, and the earth had begun its annual awakening, announcing that Easter would soon arrive. The mountains around us that had appeared so barren only a week earlier now began to take on the tint of light green as small leaves appeared. Red buds and dogwoods announced that spring had arrived and spring wildflowers awakened and peeped from the ground like a bashful small child peering from behind a door.

As we walked, Jackie suddenly stopped and said, "Look Dank. There's Old Rooster sitting on his front porch." I stared at the Reynolds home and waved at Rooster. He didn't respond. "Probably taking a nap." I said as we continued to walk down the road.

"That old man looks just like Santa Clause with his long white beard and white hair." Jackie said. "Uncle Dale once told me that Rooster really was Santa Clause."

"Your Uncle Dale was just pulling your leg, Jackie." I responded. "Rooster ain't Santa Clause. He's too skinny and besides, Santa Clause lives at the North Pole. You know that, you dumb head!"

"He might be Santa Clause." Jackie argued. "Uncle Dale don't lie and besides, Santa probably would like to live here where it's warm during the summer instead of that cold North Pole all the time. They say it's so cold up there that if you spit it freezes before it hits the ground."

I spit a thin spray of ambeer juice between my chipped front teeth and said, "Guess there would be a lot of brown icicles if I lived at the North Pole."

"Recon we'll pass on to the fourth grade, Dank?" Jackie said.

"Don't see why not....." I responded. In the distance we heard the familiar opening bell of school ring and we began to run knowing that if we were late we would be made to stand in front of the class and place our nose into a small circle drawn by the teacher on the black board. But that wouldn't compare to the punishment we would receive at home from our parents.

The day passed quickly and was one of the rare days when neither Jackie nor I were punished for some mischief. As we made our return trip to our homes, we noticed several cars and trucks at the home of Rooster Reynolds.

"I bet they're going to play cards or have a rooster fight tonight." Jackie said.

I didn't respond to Jackie's reasoning and our attention was quickly focused upon a squirrel sitting on the limb of a hickory tree. It seemed as if the squirrel was taunting us as if to say, "Here I sit and you couldn't hit me with a rock as big as a watermelon."

Jackie picked up a gravel and threw it at the squirrel. The small missile of limestone fell harmlessly beneath the limb occupied by the squirrel. We could hear it chatter as though it were laughing. Jackie threw a second, third and fourth gravel with the same results.

"Dumb old squirrel." Jackie screamed. "It's a good thing for you I got to get home and do my chores or I would knock you off that limb, cut off your tail and hang it on my bicycle. I already got the tail of your big brother on one of the handlebars."

I laughed as we walked to my home. "See you in the morning" I said as I scrambled up the steep bank in front of our house. "See you." Jackie replied as he ran up the hollow to perform the "chores" which had taken him away from his duel with the squirrel.

When I neared the back door leading into our kitchen, the smell of chicken frying tickled my nostrils and when I entered the kitchen, I saw Momma sitting at the table peeling potatoes. She looked at me and smiled, saying, "You need to change out of your school clothes and get right to your chores, Dank. We got to go down to Rooster Reynolds just as soon as your Daddy gets home."

I sat down at the table with Momma. "What's happening at Rooster's house? I saw a bunch of cars there on the way home."

Momma continued to peel the potatoes and replied, "They found the poor old man dead this morning. He was sitting on his front porch and must have died sometime last night. The sheriff called about ten o'clock this morning looking for your Daddy. When your Daddy came home a couple hours later, he had already been to the house and pronounced Rooster dead so they could move the poor thing out of that old chair. Now get to your chores. We got to go down there and help get the poor thing ready to bury."

I went to my room and changed out of my school clothes and then quickly raced outside to the feed bin. As I mixed the feed for our hogs I thought about Rooster.

Rooster, his wife and two small children had moved to our county fifty years earlier when he was in his early twenties. Some said he had moved here from Harlan County and others thought it was Letcher County. Gentry Isaacs had once told me that Rooster had killed a man during an election day argument and in order to prevent the dead man's family from exacting revenge on him or his family, he had packed up and moved a safe distance away, settling on a sixty acre farm in Owsley County where he would live the remainder of his life.

The two small children, both boys, had grown to adulthood and both had left the county long before I had been born. One had been killed in a bar room brawl in Newport and the other had been killed in a car crash somewhere in Missouri. After their deaths, some folks said Rooster's wife just seemed to waste away. She seldom smiled or visited with neighbors and spent a great deal of time sitting on her front porch in a rocking chair, staring at the hills that surrounded her home. She had died some time before we had moved into the community and had been buried on the hill behind their home.

As I made my way to the hog lot, I took a deep breath of the fresh spring air. The hogs must have sensed that I was on my way to feed them and I could hear them grunt and snort with excitement. After I had poured the feed into their feed trough, I sat down and watched them eat. While I sat, I remembered a few of the things about Rooster that our neighbors had told me.

I didn't know Rooster's given name. I had only known him as Rooster. Robert, who lived across the highway from our home had once told me that He had always been called Rooster. When I asked how he had received the nickname, Robert said he didn't really know for certain. It might have been because of the way he walked with his back straight as a pine tree and his head bobbing back and forth like a banty rooster strolling across the barnyard.

While I was watching the hogs eat and thinking of Rooster I heard Momma call for me. I stood, picked up the slop bucket and raced to the house. As I entered the kitchen, I saw Daddy sitting at the dining table with a cup of coffee in his hands. "After your Daddy finishes his coffee we're going down to Rooster's house." Momma said. "Just wear what you got on and we'll finish the chores after we get back home."

I sat down at the table with Daddy and asked, "How old was Rooster, Daddy?"

"Not really sure, Dank." He said, "Probably somewhere in his seventies. Poor man had had a lot of sorrow in his life. That may have made him seem older than he really was though." As County Coroner, Daddy was always called when there was a murder or death from an unknown cause in the county.

"How did he die?" I asked.

"His poor old heart just gave out on him. Sad thing too." Daddy answered. "We looked in the house to see if there was anything to help us know how to get in touch with any of his family but there wasn't anything we could find. Not even a Christmas card. Guess it will just be up to the folk around here to take care of his body. The County attorney is checking to see if there is a will on file in the courthouse. If there ain't, then we will have to see what we will have to do about his livestock and the rest of the farm."

"I'm ready, Bob, whenever you are." Momma said as she wiped her hands with a dishcloth and then removed her apron.

Daddy stood, taking one long, last sip of coffee.

"Here, Dank." Momma said as she handed me a platter of fried chicken. "You carry this and your Daddy and I will get the rest of the food".

The trip to Rooster's in daddy's old green ford pick-up was a short one. When we pulled into the driveway, I saw that a good many of the other neighbors had already arrived. Some children I knew were playing in the large front yard and when our truck came to a stop, Jackie Dooley came running to meet me.

"Now I know why old Rooster didn't wave at us this morning, Dank." Jackie said. "He was sitting there on that porch as dead as a door nail. I've already sat in that chair to see what it to feels like to sit in a chair that somebody was sitting in when they kicked the bucket. Didn't feel no different to me though than any other old chair."

"Slow down, little man." Daddy said to Jackie. "Here, make yourself useful and help Dank carry some of this food into the house."

Together Jackie and I made our way to the back of the house and entered the kitchen door. Several women were standing around the kitchen table talking. "Lord have mercy!" Maude Gray said as she saw the food we carried. "We got enough food here to feed Grant's army." After delivering the food, Jackie and I ran outside.

"Come on around to the front porch, Dank." Jackie said. "I want you to sit in that chair and see if you think it sits any different than the others." We raced around the house, stepped onto the porch and

I took a seat in the chair. I felt the chair arms and wiggled around on the seat and shook my head. "Don't seem any different to me." I said.

As I sat in the chair, I saw Ron and Maude Mainous come walking across the front yard. Ron and Maude lived on the farm that joined Rooster. "There comes Ron and Maude." I whispered to Jackie. Ron was a thin wisp of a man, standing about five feet eight. Maude was about the same height but was the largest woman I knew. Daddy had once told me that Maude was about two biscuits shy of four hundred pounds. She would take about ten steps and then stop, expel a long gust of air from between her thin lips, fan herself with her hand and then shake her head. Ron would also stop, look at the ground as if he were looking for something, and then begin to walk again when Maude began her next journey of ten steps.

"That is one big woman." Jackie whispered. I nodded my head in agreement. "I heard Daddy and Momma talking at supper one night." Jackie continued. "Maude went to old Doc Agers a few months ago and he told her in no uncertain terms she was going to have to lose a lot of weight. Doc asked her what she had for breakfast each morning and she told him four biscuits with gravy, ham, sausage and eggs. Then she has another four biscuits with jelly, molasses or honey. Doc told her that she could have no more than one biscuit for breakfast each morning. Made her as mad as a wet hen."

I laughed and said, "Don't seem like it's helped her any."

"No, but you ain't heard the rest of it." Jackie continued. " Ron told Uncle Dale that the next morning when Maude made breakfast, she took the largest skillet she had and made her one biscuit as large as the skillet. When she went back to Old Doc, she hadn't lost any weight and Doc asked her if she had been following the diet, he had given her. She got pretty huffy with the Doc and had him know in no uncertain terms that she did everything he asked her to do, right up to eating just one biscuit for breakfast each morning."

Jackie and I continued to watch the slow, plodding movement of Ron and Maude across the yard. As we followed their progress Jackie observed, "My Grannie Mays walked like that." and then he added, "My Daddy says that Maude wears the pants in their family."

"My daddy said the same thing." I responded. "He said that Ron and Maude hadn't been married but a few months when Ron went out one Saturday night and came home early the next morning drunk as a skunk. He slammed the doors and turned on the lights in the kitchen and yelled at Maude to get into the kitchen and fix him some breakfast. Maude came into the kitchen and saw Ron sitting at the kitchen table smoking a cigarette. She smiled at him and asked "And what does my loving husband want for breakfast this morning?" Ron slammed his hand down on the table and said, "I want eggs and sausage, biscuits and gravy and lots of hot coffee." Maude continued to smile at Ron and said, "Well, let me see what I can find for my precious little lovey-Dovey." She got a frying pan out of the cabinet and then whacked Ron right across the side of the head. Knocked him out cold and he landed on the floor of the kitchen. Maude placed the frying pan on the table, turned the kitchen light off and went back to bed. The next morning when she got up, Ron was sitting at the table with an ice pack on a big lump on his head. Maude smiled at him and asked, "And what does my loving husband want for breakfast this morning."

"That's the same thing my Daddy told me." Jackie agreed. "He said that was the last time Ron ever got out on a bender," and then we both laughed.

Daddy appeared at the side of the porch and said, "Let's go Dank. I think we are finished here." I leaped from the porch and followed Daddy to the kitchen door. "Wait here. I'll tell your Momma we're ready to go." he said.

After daddy had retrieved Momma from the kitchen we climbed into our old, green truck and began our short journey home. We had not traveled very far before Momma spoke. "I can't believe that Easter is almost here. Just look at all those wild Easter lilies. We haven't gotten our new Easter outfits. We will have to go this Saturday and do that."

As we pulled into the driveway of our home Daddy answered. "We should be able to do that without any problem."

That night I learned that the funeral for Rooster would be held the next day. It would be a community affair with the funeral being preached by Rev. Bates, the pastor of the Methodist church.

As Jackie Dooley and I walked to school the next morning, we stopped in front of Roosters' house. "Going to seem strange not seeing old Rooster sitting on that porch." Jackie. said.

"Yeah." I answered, "But I just thought of something. If we don't have Christmas this year then I guess we'll know for sure that old Rooster really was Santa Claus."

I watched closely as Jackie's facial expression changed. I had seen that look on his face before. It was a look that went from surprise to fear and then ended with a recognition of helplessness. It was the same look I had witnessed when a snapping turtle had clamped down on his finger the summer before. "That would be horrible! Don't say that, Dank!"

"Well, you said that your uncle Dale never lied and he said that Old Rooster was really Santa Claus." I replied.

Jackie's shoulders slumped and I saw moisture gathering in his eyes. He placed his lower lip between his teeth and slowly shook his head from side to side. I placed my hand on his shoulder and said, "Don't worry, Jackie. Maybe your uncle Dale was wrong. Maybe he was just saying something that someone else had told him. We'll walk up to his house tonight and ask him."

We continued our slow journey to school.

That evening I walked with Jackie to his house. We stepped onto the front porch and Jackie said, "Wait here Dank and I'll be right back."

Jackie went into the house. He stayed only a few minutes and then came bursting through the screen door to where I sat on the porch. "Let's go down to the woodshed." he said.

Jackie and I raced off the sloping hill where his house set and down to the woodshed that set next to the dirt road. "I've got my bicycle in here." Jackie said. "You can ride Patty's bike if you want. It's an old girls' bike but no one will see you riding it and it rides pretty good to be a girls' bike."

Soon we were riding the bikes up the Tincher Fork of the Creek. Easter flags, dogwoods, and red buds lined the side of the road. Jackie skid to a stop on his bicycle and pointed to the weathered bones of an old chimney. "Mama and Daddy used to live in that house that stood here." Jackie said. "It burned to the ground when my oldest brother was a baby and they moved to where we live now."

Soon we arrived at the home of Jackie's uncle. It was a large two-story white frame home with a long front porch. The window frames, door frames, and shutters that decorated the house were all painted black. We laid our bicycles on the ground and stepped up onto the porch and Jackie yelled through the screen door, "Is anybody here?"

I heard the sound of steps coming to the door and saw the smiling face of Jackie's Aunt Bessie. "Well Lordy, Lordy look who's here." She said.

Bessie open the screen door and said, "You boys get on in this house."

"We come to talk to Uncle Dale about something mighty important." Jackie answered. "Is he home?"

"Why I think he's down at the barn, mending some harnesses." Bessie replied. "Thank you, Aunt Bessie." Jackie said and he turned from the door and leaped off the porch. "Come on Dank" he yelled as he raced toward the barn. I obediently followed behind.

We found Jackie's uncle sitting at the side of the barn on a long homemade bench with a harness laying across his knees. "Well look at what the dogs drug in." Dale said. "What brings you boys up here?"

"We come to ask you a very important question Uncle Dale." Jackie responded. "It's about the most important question in this whole wide world."

"Well I'm mighty humbled that you would want to ask me such an important question. I have always told your aunt Bessie from the time we got married that I was about the smartest man on God's earth and now you have just proved it right. Let me hear this important question."

"Was old Rooster Reynolds really Santa Claus?" Jackie asked.

Dale looked at me and smiled. He took the harness off his knee and laid it on the ground. He then reached in his hip pocket and took out a twist of homegrown chewing tobacco. Slowly he removed a case pocketknife from his front pocket, cut a slice of tobacco from the twist, and placed it into his mouth. "Well given the circumstances I would say that is a very important question. If old Rooster really was Santa Claus then that would mean that we are all left hung out to dry."

I looked at Jackie. His lower lip began to tremble.

"But I've got it from a good source that old Rooster really wasn't Santa Claus at all. Do you know how I know that?" Jackie and I both shook our heads "No."

"Well, you see this harness here. This harness ain't for any old ordinary work mule. It ain't even for a fine bred saddle horse. This here harness is really for Santa's reindeer." I saw Jackie's eyes grow large and his mouth flew open. "Yes sir the old boy up at the North Pole sent word to me this morning by one of his elves that he needed a good set of harness for one of his reindeer and he knew that I was about the best harness maker in all these parts so that's what I'm doing. Don't really know which reindeer will wear it but I do know that all the other reindeer will be jealous of it."

"I knew it! I knew it!" Jackie said as he twirled around and around like a little girl and then slapped me on the back. "Thank you Uncle Dale. Thank you! Thank you!" Jackie screamed. And then looking at me he said, "Let's go Dank!"

We ran back to the bicycles, mounted them, and then rode like the wind back to Jackie's home.

The next week passed quickly. People within the community busied themselves with spring chores. Gardens were plowed, tobacco beds burned, and following a long, hard winter repairs made. The Dogwood and red buds were in full bloom. The oak, maple, hickory, Sycamore, and other trees that covered the mountains around us began to clothe themselves with light green leaves that would rival the pine and spruce which had ruled supreme during the winter.

On Easter Sunday we dressed ourselves in our new clothes, climbed into our pickup truck and began our journey to church. I sat next to the passenger door and rolled the door window half open. "Dank! Roll that window back up!" Momma said. "That wind is going to mess my hair up!" I quickly obeyed.

When we arrived at the church a large number of people had

already gathered. Small groups of men stood in the churchyard talking, whittling, and laughing. They were all dressed in new overalls or dress pants and white shirts and each wore a hat. Children, dressed in new Easter clothes, were playing tag.

"Now Dank," Momma said, "I don't want you getting your new clothes all messed up. We're going up to your Grannies after church and you will have plenty of time to play then."

I walked slowly with Momma to the front of the church and watched as she made her way up the steps and into the building. I then turned to join the other children as they played.

The church bell rang and the men placed their knives into their pockets, removed the chews of tobacco from their mouths and began to move slowly toward the church. The children also stopped their play and ran up the steps and into the building.

As I entered the church I saw where Momma was sitting and joined her. Soon Daddy entered the church and made his way to the Deacon's bench and took a seat. Millard Green walked to the pulpit, smiled and said, "Everybody stand and let us begin the service by singing, He Arose."

As the congregation began to sing, I allowed my eyes to wander around the room. I focused first upon Aunt Martha Biggs. She was a small, frail woman well into her 80s. Her hair was as white as a Christmas snow. Her head was tilted slightly to the back as it moved from side to side. Her eyes were gazing upward as though she were looking through the ceiling of the church and upon the mansions of heaven. Her small hands marked by the passing of time were held in front of her and moving as though she were directing a heavenly choir.

My attention was next given to Willie Moore. He was a short rotund man with a balding head. There was a time not too long ago when Willie loved his whiskey more than his family. Since he had been saved in a revival meeting a couple years earlier, Willy had abstained from strong drink and became a model husband and father. At this time the only stain upon his life appeared to be the brown splotches of tobacco juice upon his white shirt. His eyes were also looking upward and his large body swayed back and forth.

Standing next to Willie was Bige Williams. Bige was leaning slightly forward with his large hands gripping the back of the pew in front of him. He was not singing. He didn't seem to be listening to the music or the voices around him. Although he was standing in the New Hope Church on Easter Sunday, it seemed as though Bige had been carried by his mind to another place.

After the congregation had finished singing "He Arose" everyone took a seat. I watched closely as Patsy Biggs walked to the pulpit. Patsy was a senior in high school and a local celebrity. She had a large Gibson guitar hanging on the strap around her neck. Some people said that Patsy had been singing from the time she came out of her mother's womb. I had heard Mama say that Patsy Biggs would become the next Patsy Cline.

Patsy looked at the congregation and smiled. Her large brown eyes seemed to twinkle and her long chestnut brown hair that reached to her waist seemed to glisten as she began to sing, "I come to the garden alone while the dew is still on the roses." The entire congregation became as quiet as mice. The babies that had been fretful became silent. The children that had been restless became still. Every eye was on Patsy and every ear was open to hear the voice that everyone believed would one day be heard on the Grand Ol' Opry.

When Patsy finished her song there was a mixture of applause and shouts of "Amen" by the congregation. Preacher Barnes stepped to the pulpit. His head was covered with thick white hair and he wore a black suit. I had never seen preacher Barnes wear anything but a black suit. I wondered if that was the only suit he owned. He laid his large black Bible on the pulpit. His large callused hands gripped the sides of the pulpit as his piercing black eyes examined the congregation.

As preacher Barnes opened his mouth and began to speak the front doors of the church were thrown open with a loud crash and it sounded as if a mule was racing down the aisle of the church. When I first heard the sound I thought that Benny Miller was pulling another prank. Last fall, when fodder shocks decorated the landscape, and the church was in the midst of a revival meeting, Benny and some of his fellow pranksters had borrowed a neighbors pony, brought it to church, and in the middle of the preacher's sermon had brought it into the church, slapped it on the rump and laughed loudly as the pony galloped down the aisle to the pulpit. Benny spent two weeks in jail for disturbing the peace.

I kept my eyes focused on the aisle fully expecting to see another pony, mule, or cow come racing down the aisle. I was surprised. It wasn't a pony. It wasn't a mule. It wasn't a cow. It was Maude Mainous. This was truly an Easter miracle. Maude Mainous could run! It wasn't a graceful run and I had never seen anyone run quite like this before but no one could deny that Maude was running.

Maude ran all the way down the aisle and fell on her knees in front of the pulpit. She lifted her short pudgy arms above her head and said, "He is alive. Oh, dear Jesus, he's alive! I just seen him! He ain't dead! He's done come back from the grave!"

Preacher Barnes came from behind the pulpit and knelt beside Maude. He placed his large hand on Maude's shoulder and said, "Hallelujah! Yes, Sister Maude he is alive! Praise the Lord! Jesus is alive!"

Maude's short, fleshy arm darted out and caught preacher Barnes in his chest, sending him flying backwards. "No you idiot! I ain't talking about Jesus! Everybody knows Jesus is alive! I'm talking about Rooster Reynolds! That old man has come back from the grave! I just seen him!"

It took her a few tries but Maude struggled to her feet and turned to face the congregation. Large beads of sweat were on her face and her voice trembled as she began to speak.

"Ron and me were on our way to church this morning and we took a shortcut across Rooster's pasture field. We come by the foot of that little knoll of the hill where Rooster is buried and I heard somebody whistling. Ron and me stopped and looked up at the graveyard. That's when we seen him. He was standing there and had his hand resting on that big old sandstone tombstone that marks his grave. He turned and saw me and Ron and he raised his hand from the tombstone and waved at us. He made like he was going to come off the hill and walk down to where Ron and me stood. That is when my head told my legs to save my body. I started to run with Ron right behind me."

Maude paused and looked around at the congregation. She had a look on her face that I had seen only a few times before. I saw it on the face of Jackie Dooley the day that his father had told him that Tucker, his old Redbone hound had died. I had also seen it on the face of Skinny Johnson. I had been at the store when Skinny arrived and gathered some needed items from the store shelves. He had taken them to the counter and was preparing to pay when he felt in his pockets and discovered that he had lost his money somewhere between his house and the store.

"Oh, my dear Lord! I've done run off and left Ron! I've got to go find him!" Maude hunched her shoulders and put her arms in a running mode and prepared to run back to the Reynolds farm when Ron appeared at the church door. He half staggered and half stumbled down the aisle. Maude met him halfway. Ron bent over, placing his long scrawny hands on his small knobby knees and between deep breaths said, "It's………… true…….. Old…….. Rooster…….. is………. back…….. from………. the…….. grave…..." All of the years of smoking had given Ron a wheezing sound that reminded me of the sound the bellows made when I watched Robert Bowman make shoes for his mules.

Maude hugged Robert. Gertrude Wilson walked to where Ron was standing. She had a fan in her hand. It had been given to the church by the King Justice Funeral Home at the last revival. Gertrude began to fan Ron as he continued to talk.

"Who….. would…… have……. thought……. it……. could…….. happen?……. Who would…….. have dreamed…… anyone…….. could shake off………. the shackles of death………. and come back…….. to the living?…… But it happened!….. I seen it with my own eyes."

Ron raised to an upright position as Maude kept her tight grip on his waist. Preacher Barnes had also raised himself from the dusty church floor and made his way to the pulpit. "All right people," Preacher Barnes said, "Let's all get settled back in our seats."

Maude helped Ron to a pew and gently sat him down. The

congregation continued to stare at Ron and Maude as she took a seat next to him. It seemed as though no one was interested in the sermon that preacher Barnes was delivering. Perhaps sensing that he did not have the attention of the congregation, preacher Barnes finished his message in less than 15 minutes. The congregation stood and sang one more hymn. Preacher Barnes then asked Bruce Sizemore to close the service in prayer. Bruce approached the pulpit and in a loud voice asked everyone to bow their heads. He then began his prayer, "O Lord God in heaven you have given us an Easter that we will always remember. Bless us now we pray. Amen."

I had never heard Bruce Sizemore pray such a short prayer. His prayers usually competed with preacher Barnes' sermon in the length. After the prayer people began to leave the church. Outside they collected into small groups. I knew that at least on this day their conversations were not about family or crops or politics or the latest scandals within the community.

After about 15 minutes the groups began to dissipate as individuals left the church ground and made their way home. Some would be expecting company to arrive and others would become the guests at the homes of friends or relatives as they celebrated an Easter Dinner. I did learn at a later time that a group of men from the church had traveled to the Reynolds farm and did a search of the cemetery, house, and outbuildings. It was their judicial findings that the grave of Rooster was intact and that everything on the farm seemed to be in its proper place.

A couple weeks passed without any new sightings of Rooster. Although Rooster was out of sight he certainly was not out of mind. The appearance of Rooster on Easter Sunday was the main topic of conversation when neighbors would visit each other, men would gather at the store, ladies would gather for their weekly quilting meetings or families would sit and talk in the evening. Some of the conversations were of a more serious nature while others were spoken with a smile on their lips. The community appeared to be divided into two groups: those who believed that if the grave of Rooster were opened his body would not be found and those who believed that Maude and Ron had been the victims of a community jokester.

I had walked to the store on Saturday morning. There was the usual gathering of men from within the community who had taken their seats on the long wooden bench that set on the front porch. I went into the store and bought an RC Cola and returned to the front porch taking a seat on the edge of the porch and letting my legs dangle lazily. As the conversation of the men shifted from weather to politics and then to local gossip I saw Willard Mason walking toward the store. He seemed to be in a hurry. As he stepped up onto the porch he said, "Well you ain't going to believe it! You just sure ain't going to believe it!"

Taylor Marcum said, "What ain't we going to believe Willard? I'll bet you caught a bass out of the Sturgeon Creek that measured 6 inches between its eyes." Taylor laughed and then slapped his knee with his thin calloused hand.

"No! It ain't got nothing to do with fishing or hunting or anything else that you fellas would know anything about but it is about Rooster Reynolds." Willard yelled. "But now if you fellows ain't interested in hearing I'll just mosey on down the road."

I watched the faces of the men as they looked at each other and finally focused their gaze on Taylor. There was silence. Then the silence was broken as Taylor spoke again, "Well don't just stand there! Tell us what this big news is that you've got that we won't believe."

Taylor smiled and then began to speak. "I just heard from the horse's mouth that tall Jim Botner - it wasn't Shorty Jim or Red Jim or Black Jim Botner, it was Tall Jim Botner- anyways, he was on his way home yesterday evening. He had been helping Bige Gray build his new smokehouse and it was about 3 o'clock in the afternoon when he decided he would take a shortcut across the Reynolds place. As he was walking along all sweaty and tired he heard someone whistling. It was a familiar whistle he had heard lots of times before and so he looked up to where the sound was coming from and he saw the back of a man standing up in the cemetery. He kept on walking, but he also kept looking at that graveyard. Anyway, he said that the man turned around and looked right straight at him and he would swear on a stack of Bibles that the man was Rooster Reynolds. Old Rooster waved at him and smiled. Well it goes without saying that Tall Jim got a fresh boost of energy and he took off running, but he dropped his hacksaw, hammer and level. He said that any man brave enough to go in and get them could have them."

Taylor stood to his feet and said, "I could sure use a good hand saw, hammer and level. Who wants to ride up to the Reynolds place with me?"

Andy Burch stood and said, "I'm game enough to go with you." We watched as the two men slid into Taylor's old Chevrolet pickup and drove off.

After about an hour the two men returned. They climbed from the old pickup and walked up to the store porch holding in their hands a handsaw, hammer and level. Andy spoke, "We just got back from the Reynolds place and we found these tools just like Willard said. But we didn't hear nobody whistling. We didn't see Old Rooster prancing around in the graveyard. We didn't see anything except these tools and a few old crows scratching around in last year's corn patch."

Another three weeks passed and from time to time people would say they had seen or heard unusual things on the Reynolds farm. Simeon Green had heard the sound of Rooster's whistle coming from the tobacco barn. Late one evening Dorcie Turner had seen old Rooster sitting on his front porch. Susie Farmer had seen a light moving from the living room to an upstairs bedroom late one night. Most people had decided to detour around the Reynolds farm or turn their heads if they were passing by.

One Thursday I had come home from school. It was the last day of my third year of formal education. I looked forward to a long summer. As we sat at the supper table Daddy said, "I talked with the county attorney today and it seems as if some of Rooster's family has been found. They were living in Harlan County. They are supposed to come by his office in the morning and he is going to issue them a deed to the Reynolds property. But we do have a problem. It seems as if so many people have heard or seen Rooster that he doesn't know if he can issue a deed or not. Even though he was dead and we buried him all proper and legal there might be some question as to whether he is dead or not. The county attorney wants me to get some men and go to the farm and dig up Roosters coffin and see if he is really in it or not. If his body ain't there, then he must be resurrected or something. It's really causing the county attorney to do an awful lot of researching. I'll have to go down to the crossroads in the morning and find the Biggs Brothers and get them to help dig up the coffin."

Early the next morning after we had eaten breakfast I climbed into daddy's truck and rode with him to the store. He let me out and said, "Dank I'm going on down to the crossroads and find the Biggs Brothers. You stay out of trouble and don't let them old men talk you into doing something you shouldn't do."

I climbed out of the truck and walked to the front porch of the store. I took a seat on the bench next to Andy Burch. Andy was whittling on a piece of Cedar. From time to time he would spit a thin spray of tobacco juice onto the gravel covered ground next to the porch. Sometimes his spit would hit the edge of the porch and splatter, leaving a wet Brown stain. "Where's your Daddy off to Dank?"

"He's going to get the Biggs Brothers and they're going to dig up old Rooster's body this morning." I replied.

Andy stopped quickly and looked at me. "You don't say!" He said. "Now why on God's green earth would they want to do something like that? Just don't seem natural. A man's sleep of death shouldn't ever be disturbed. At least not until Jesus splits the skies and old Gabriel sounds his horn at the resurrection." Even though I knew the reasoning I shrugged my shoulders and shook my head from side to side.

In a few minutes I saw a large black Oldsmobile pull up at the gas pump in front of the store. A young man climbed out of the driver's side of the car, stepped up onto the porch, said "Howdy Fellas." He then entered the building. "The young feller has been here before," Andy said, "but I have no idea who he is."

Conley, the owner of the store, came to the door. "Dank" he said "would you fill up that Oldsmobile with gas for me and then just holler and tell me how much it was."

I walked to the gas pump, turned the knob, opened the gas cover, unscrewed the lid, and began to fill the car up with gas. As the car was being filled with gas I reached into a bucket of water sitting next to the gas pump, took out a sponge, and started to clean the windshield. As I looked into the car I dropped the sponge and stepped back. Sitting in the passenger seat as big as day was Rooster Reynolds. He smiled at me. He rolled his window down and stuck his head out and said, "You all right son?" I couldn't speak. I just continued to stare. He opened the car door and stepped out onto the gravel. I heard a noise on the front porch. I turned and saw Andy laying sprawled out on the porch floor. Conley stepped to the door looked at Andy laying as still as a mouse on the porch and said, "What in tarnation is going on out here?" Conley then turned his gaze toward me and then toward Rooster. His mouth flew open and his legs began to tremble just like a sinner on judgment day.

The young man who had been the driver of the Oldsmobile appeared behind Conley and gently nudged him aside, rushed out onto the porch and let his gaze rest on Rooster. "Are you all right, Pappy?" he yelled as he rushed off the porch and ran to the car. "I'm fine." Rooster answered, "But whoever that feller is on the porch don't look like he's doing too well."

The young man looked at Andy still lying sprawled out on the store porch, rushed back to the porch and knelt next to Andy. "It's all right Mister." he said. "I'm a Doctor." He smacked Andy on each jaw and then asked Andy if he was feeling any pain in his arms or chest. Rooster walked past me to the edge of the porch and watched as the young man cared for Andy. The young man felt Andy's forehead, neck, arms, chest and legs and then looking at Conley said, "I think he must have fainted. Come over here and help me sit him up." Conley's eyes remained focused on Rooster and was oblivious to the young man's directions. "Mister!" the young man shouted, "Come on over here and help me sit this man up." Conley looked at the young man and then Andy and walked slowly to where they were. After kneeling next to Andy, Conley's eyes again focused on Rooster as he helped the young man bring Andy to a sitting position.

As I watched all the events taking place, I heard the sound of a familiar truck engine approaching the store. I knew from instinct that it was my Daddy. I had listened for that familiar sound many days as I waited for Daddy to get home from work. I turned and saw the truck approaching the store. I rushed out to the edge of the road and waved both arms in the air as a signal of distress. Daddy saw me and he came to a screeching stop, angling the truck around the Oldsmobile and coming to a stop near the store porch. I saw that he had Bill and Ben Biggs in the cab of the truck with him.

Daddy opened the driver's side door and stepped from the truck. The Biggs brothers opened the passenger side door and began to run across a large field next to the store. Daddy's eyes were focused on Rooster and approaching Rooster slowly, Daddy, his eyes wide in amazement, reached out and touched Rooster's arm. "Rooster? Is that really you Rooster?" Daddy stuttered. Rooster looked at Daddy and smiled. "No. I ain't Rooster. I'm his brother.... his twin brother." Behind Daddy and Rooster, I could see Andy, sitting up and staring at the two men. Conley was also staring at Daddy and Rooster and the young man began to laugh hysterically.

After the commotion died down, we all entered the store and bought a soda pop and talked. Rooster's twin brother was named Floyd and Rooster's name had been Fred. He told us something of Rooster's past and how he had come to live in Owsley County. At an early age Rooster had gotten his nickname because he was as game as a man could be, always getting into fights and unafraid to tackle any man no matter how much larger than Rooster that man might have been. Rooster's family was very prosperous in Harlan County and heavily involved in politics. As a young man, Rooster had been helping his father campaign for County Judge and was soliciting votes at one of the county precincts on Election Day. He had gotten into an argument with some of his father's political enemies and the argument evolved into something more than a fist fight. Pistols had been drawn and Rooster killed two men, leaving them lying on the precinct ground, and then rode calmly away on his horse. The courts had found Rooster innocent of murder on the grounds of self-defense, but the family knew his days were numbered if he continued to live in Harlan County. The families of the murdered men wouldn't rest until they fulfilled the Biblical adage of "an eye for an eye and a tooth for a tooth." Rooster's family had encouraged him to leave Harlan County. Rooster had never returned to Harlan County again. Even when his father and mother had died, Rooster had stayed away.

When Floyd had heard from the Harlan County Attorney that Rooster had died, he had made a visit to the Reynolds farm on Easter Sunday and visited Rooster's grave and then made other visits from time to time after that. On this visit he would meet with the County Attorney and arrange for the settlement of Rooster's estate.

As we left the store, I climbed into the passenger seat of Daddy's truck. "Floyd, I'll meet with you all at the County Attorney's Office and get this matter of Rooster's resurrection settled." Daddy yelled. Floyd smiled and waved as he and his grandson entered their Oldsmobile.

Daddy and I travelled in silence. I had lowered the passenger door window and allowed the wind to brush against my face. I looked closely at the neat homes and cultivated fields of our neighbors along the way.

Then Daddy spoke. "Well Dank, it has been quite an interesting day. I guess now everybody will stop talking about the resurrection of Rooster Reynolds and find something new to talk about."

Then there was silence again until Daddy said. "You know Dank, I kind of hoped that the stories about Old Roosters rising from the grave might have been true. He was a mighty good man and an awful good neighbor. I don't doubt that some day when Gabriel blows his horn Old Rooster is going to raise up from that piece of earth where he sleeps and start whistling as he rises up into the clouds."

Daddy reached over and turned on the radio and we heard the sound of Hank Williams as he sorrowfully declares,

These shabby shoes I'm wearin' all
Are full of holes and nails
And brother if I stepped on a worn out dime
I bet a nickel I could tell you if it was heads or tails.
I'm not gonna worry wrinkles in my brow

Cause nothin's ever gonna be alright now
No matter how I struggle and strive
I'll never get out of this world alive.

Daddy glanced over at me and said, "Well, ain't that something, Dank. Seems strange that song would be on the radio right at this time, doesn't it. Well, maybe the Good Maker is trying to remind us of something."

I nodded my head and we drove in silence as I thought of the momentary resurrection of Rooster Reynolds.

Chapter 5

Fireball and Willie

"This is the best day ever" I thought to myself as I stood at the edge of our yard, preparing to slide down the steep bank which would place me at the side of the road in front of our home.

I continued to think. "My third year of school ended last Friday, my morning chores are done, the sun is shining bright and I got a whole quarter in my pocket to spend at the store."

At that moment I heard the sound of an approaching car. It was coming down the winding gravel road and I could tell it was moving fast. I turned to see Fireball Goosey in his 1951 Ford with flames painted on the front and down the sides approaching me. His radio was turned up to the highest volume and I could hear Carl Perkins singing "Blue Suede Shoes. I could see the head of Fireball moving back and forth as he sang along with the radio, "You can burn my house, steal my car, drink my liquor from an old fruit jar….. " as he raced by me.

"I kind of doubt he would let anyone steal his car" I thought to myself. Fireball was a moonshine runner for his daddy and uncle and that car was known all too well by the sheriffs in eight counties. The whole county knew what Fireball did for a living, but he was well liked by everyone. He was mild mannered and respectful, saying sir or mam to the older folk, laughing and joking with the kids, and helpful to anyone who might need his help. He had long black hair that he kept oiled and combed back into a ducktail. His shirt collar was always turned up in the back and he dressed in blue jeans with sharp toed cowboy boots.

I slid over the bank and onto the road, dusted the backside of my jeans off and started to walk with a small boy's stride, carefully examining the road in front of me. I hadn't walked very far until I heard a voice call my name. "Dank… Hey Dank." I stopped in my tracks and looked around. "Down here, Dank." the voice said. I turned my eyes to the creek that ran beside the road and saw Willie Green standing barefoot in the creek. "Come on down here and help me." Willie said.

Willie was a tall, thin man about thirty years old with red hair and a freckled face. He wasn't ugly but he wasn't known for his good looks either. Willie usually wore blue jeans and a plaid shirt but today he was wearing blue dress pants and a white shirt.

Willie lived alone in Gum Hollow. He owned about forty acres and raised tobacco and corn and worked part time jobs doing whatever he could find to do. He also raised cattle and bred mules as a sideline and seemed to make a pretty good living.

"Help you do what?" I asked

"Durn it, Dank! Come on down here and help me look for a ring I lost in this creek. I was walking along this road, minding my own business and looking at my ring when that fool Fireball Goosey came down this road like a bat out of hades and might near run right over me. I had to jump down into this creek to keep from getting killed and I lost my ring."

I slid down yet another bank to the creek and started to help look for the ring. "What kind of ring was it?" I asked Willie.

"It's a woman's engagement ring." Willie answered.

"Engagement ring?" I asked

"Ain't that what I just said? I shore hope your eyes are better than your hearing, Dank." Willie chided. "Oh, dear sweet Jesus," And then Willie prayed the prayer of a desperate man in the trembling voice of a man who was beside himself with sheer desperation. "I know I ain't been much of a man and I ain't never done nothing but run all over this country, drinking and gambling and doing all such stuff as that, but, dear precious Lord, if you will just let me find this ring, I'll get myself right to church next Sunday. Yes sweet Jesus, I'll even get all my friends to come to church with me"

I interrupted Willie's prayer with a question, "Where did you fall into the creek?"

"I don't know." Willie said. "I was too busy trying to save my life to notice where I jumped into the creek. It's right around in here somewhere. I had it in my hand and when I fell over into the creek, it just popped right out of my hand but I know it's right here…. somewhere right here. You find that ring, Dank and I'll give you a whole fifty cents."

I looked at the creek bank again and saw where I had slid into the creek and then at another place where I figured Willie had come sliding from the road and into the cool water. I walked to the spot where the sliding marks led to the creek and began to look for the ring. Before long, I saw the shiny silver ring with a small diamond glistening in the water and picked it up, holding it in my hand while Willie with his back turned to me continued to look under rocks in the creek for his precious ring.

"Willie, you did say you'd give me a whole fifty cents if I found the ring, didn't you?" I said.

"Good heavens, Dank!" Willie responded. "My old grandpa can hear better than you…. YES! YES! YES! I told you that I'd give you a whole fifty cents, now keep on looking." Willie screamed.

"I don't know, Willie, but I believe if that ring was as important to me as it seems to be to you, I would even give somebody a whole dollar if they found it for me." I suggested.

"Dank, you find that ring and I'll give you a dollar….. A whole dollar." Willie agreed.

I waited a couple of minutes and then announced, "Well bless my soul, Willie! Is this what we're looking for?"

Willie turned and faced me, his eyes upon the small ring I held in my hand. A smile came to his lips and he rushed at me, jerking the ring from my hand and then kissed it several times.

"Oh, praise be to Jesus…. And thank you Dank….. I've found my ring that I'm going to place on the beautiful little hand of my Ethel Mae." Willie rejoiced.

"Ethel Mae? Ethel May Wilder? Are you sweet on Ethel Mae Wilder?" I asked.

Ethel Mae was part of a large family that lived about a mile from my home. They were as poor as Job's turkey but they were good people and honest. Ethel Mae was the oldest child yet at home. She would earn money for the family by doing housecleaning, and she wasn't above working in the tobacco fields along with the men. She was a pretty girl but I had never known of her dating anyone. Seems like she never had time for courting with the family needing her to help provide for their needs.

Willie and I climbed up the steep bank of the creek to the road. "I swear to goodness," Willie said. "If I ever get hold of that Fireball Goosey, I'm going to ring his thin little neck just like a chicken. That idiot almost killed me….Why Dank, worse than that, he almost made me lose my ring. If I hadn't found this here ring, I would have gone through my whole life as a bachelor and died all alone with no one to mourn my passing."

I listened as Willie talked and then interrupted. "Willie, you do remember saying that you would give me a whole dollar if I found your ring, don't you?"

Willie stopped and looked at me, "Why sure I remember, Dank! But we'll have to wait until we get to the store. I ain't got nothing less than a five-dollar bill. I'll get some change and pay you…. Let it be said, Willie Green always pays his debts and is a man of his word. Don't you ever forget that Dank."

"All right, Willie." I said, "I won't ever forget it."

As we neared the store, I saw Fireball's car setting at the gas pumps and Fireball was standing, staring up into the sky, while filling his gas tank.

"Willie?" I said "There's Fireball. Now's your chance to ring his neck like a chicken. Unless you want to wait until you get some change and pay me my dollar. That might be the best thing to do, don't you think Willie?"

I may have been nine years old, but I was old enough to know that Fireball would kill Willie if he started anything, and I might get to see someone killed but I would be a dollar poorer for witnessing it. Fireball was basically a good-natured man, unless he got mad and then he would tackle anything that threatened him. Some people said that is how he got his nickname, because when he got mad, you could see the fire jump right out of the balls of his eyes.

"Well, I guess it wouldn't hurt none." Willie responded. "I guess he didn't mean anything by it, but I'm going to tell him that he almost killed me and he better not ever let that happen again."

Willie and I walked into the store and I patiently waited for Willie to get change from Mrs. Emma, the store owner's wife. Fireball entered the store still singing, "Well you can knock me down, step on my face, slander my name all over the place. Do anything that you wanna do, but, uh-uh, honey, lay off of them shoes.....""

Willie handed me a dollar and Fireball said, "Why howdy Willie. I ain't seen you in forever and a day. What you been up to?"

"Well that explains it" Willie said.

"Explains what?" Fireball asked.

"That explains why you pretty near ran right over me a few minutes ago..... Up the road there. You mean you didn't see me when you came around that curve just like you was being chased by some Constable. Why, Fireball, I had to jump right out of the road and into the creek to keep from getting killed."

"Well, Willie, old boy. I sure didn't see you and I am right sorry... I sure am.... Are you all right?

"I am now. I lost my engagement ring in the creek and Dank here found it for me, or else, Fireball, I would be as mad as a wet hen right now." Willie answered.

"Engagement ring? What's that you say.... Who you going to give an engagement ring to, Willie?" Mrs. Emma asked.

Willie smiled, blushed and said. "Mrs. Emma, I'm giving this here ring to the prettiest girl in the county..... Ethel Mae Wilder. I'm going down to see her daddy right now and then give it to her and ask her to marry me, if she'll have me."

"Well, you won't find her at home, Willie!" Mrs. Emma replied.

"Why, is she doing some house cleaning for somebody? I can go there I guess." Willie said.

"Why, no, Willie. She was just in here a little while ago. Her daddy was taking her to town to catch a Black Brothers Bus for Richmond and then a big old Greyhound bus to Dayton. Her sister up there has got Ethel Mae a job lined up."

I saw Willie's jaw drop and his body trembled. "Oh, for Pete's sake, Mrs. Emma. Say it ain't so. Please, Mrs. Emma say my sweet Ethel Mae ain't up and leaving the county."

"Well Willie, I could say it, but that wouldn't change anything. In fact, she's probably on that Black Brothers Bus about now and getting ready to head off to Richmond."

"Well that ain't going to happen. I'm going to stop her if it's the last thing I do." Willie said. "Fireball, you got to help me. They ain't no faster car in this whole county than that Ford of yours setting out there. You got to take me to Richmond right now...."

"Well I don't know, Willie." Fireball began, "I got a big job tonight... Have to go all the way to Hazard."

"Listen, Fireball.... You might near killed me a little while ago and this is the least that you could do for a man that you almost sent to the arms of the Lord." Willie insisted.

"Welllllll" Fireball drawled. "I guess it would only be the right thing to do. But we have to hurry and this is going to be the ride of your life."

"I sure would like to go to Richmond, Willie" I said.

"No sir.... Ain't no way on God's good earth I'm taking Dank with us." Fireball said. "His daddy would skin both of us Willie, and then hang our hides on his barn door for everyone to see."

"He's right, Dank." Willie agreed. "Your Daddy would kill us both. We know what a dangerous man he is when he gets mad."

"Daddy won't care..... I promise he won't say nothing at all, will he Mrs. Emma?" I pleaded.

"No, Bob won't say nothing. He knows Dank has a good head on his shoulders and can take care of himself. Bob and Emma have raised all their boys that way." Mrs. Emma confirmed.

"Well, but you better tell that to Bob if he tries to kill us." Fireball replied.

"Come on… time's wasting and my sweet little Ethel Mae is on her way to leaving me forever if we don't get going." Willie cried as he ran to the front door of the store.

"Let's go Dank!" Fireball commanded. "Ain't nothing in this world worse than a lovesick fool and you're going to get to ride all the way to Richmond with one."

By the time Fireball and I reached the car, Willie was already sitting in the front seat, holding the small ring in his hands and staring at it with a sad, heartbroken look on his face. He reminded me of an old sad eyed mule that Daddy once owned.

Fireball opened the driver's door. Pulled up the seat and let me climb into the back. Fireball took his seat, closed the door and started the engine.

"Hang on boys. We're going through Ida Mae and Heidleburg, out the Yellow Rock Road to Hatton Holler Hill….. We should get to Richmond well ahead of that Black Brother's Bus." Fireball said confidently.

Fireball turned the car onto the gravel road and sped away, flinging gravels and turning up the radio to its full volume. I had never ridden in a moonshine runner's car before and I felt like a nineteen year old.

Just before we reached Ida Mae I heard a siren. I looked through the back window and saw Merida Smith, a constable, following us. He had his blue light flashing.

"Good Heaven's Fireball!" Willie said. I hope you ain't got no shine in the trunk of this thing. If you do, you better push that pedal to the floor and get us out of here. The county line ain't that far away and Olde Merida can't go past that."

"No, ain't got nothing to hide. We better pull over and make old Merida's day." Fireball said as he pulled to the side of the road.

I watched as Merida climbed out of his old Chevrolet coupe, pulled up his pants and walked toward us. He was a short, fat man and his belly hung over a well-worn black belt. His little round face was covered by a brown felt hat that sat tilted precariously on his head. I could see his pistol sticking out of his front pants pocket. He walked slowly to the driver's side of the car.

Merida looked into the driver's window and said, "Well, goodness gracious, now what have we got here? Why, I do believe its Fireball Goosey, and he's in a real hurry to get somewhere fast. Who's that with you Fireball?" Merida said as he gazed at Willie. "Mercy, mercy! It don't get no better than this." Merida continued. "I think I spy Willie Green in there with you, Fireball. You must be giving that boy some shine running lessons."

"No, you're wrong Merida." Fireball laughed. "I'm giving the shine running lessons to Dank, back there…. You know Dank, don't you Merida…. He's the County Coroner's boy."

Merida looked back at me and I saw both his jaws drop.

"Listen, Merida." Willie spoke. "We're on a mission. We gotta get to Richmond fast. The love of my life is going to be lost forever if we don't get to Richmond before that Black Brothers Bus. Now if you're going to give us a ticket or something then hurry up and give it to us…. We got to be back on our way."

"Fireball, you ain't trying to pull a fast one on me, are you? Are you Sure you ain't got no whine in that trunk?" Merida asked.

"No Merida, I ain't got no shine in my trunk. Do you think I'm a crazy man? Wait, I better change that. Do you believe I'm a man who wants to die? You know Bob would kill me right on the spot if I had his boy and shine both in this car at the same time." Fireball replied.

"That's kinda what I figured." Merida said. "All right, but who is this love of Willie's life." Merida inquired.

"For crying out loud, Merida, It's Ethel Mae Wilder. She's on her way to Richmond in that Black Brother's Bus and we got to catch her before she gets on that big old Greyhound bus for Dayton, Ohio. Now, please, Merida, a heartbroken man is begging you, please let us get going." Willie whined.

"Well, Willie. Never let it be said that Merida Smith stands between a man and his true love. You boys go on and I'll do you one better. I'll call ahead to Lee County and tell them that you are three men on a mission and to not stop this car for nothing at all. I'll even ask them to call on down to Estill County and Madison County for you." Merida said.

"God bless you, Merida" Willie said. "You are a good man, Merida and I sure aim to vote for you in the next election."

Merida smiled, patted the side of the car and then turned to walk away

Fireball pulled the car into low gear, gunned the engine and then sped away, once again throwing gravels behind us. I watched as Merida jumped and grabbed the back of his legs, feeling the sting of the gravels as they pounded his backside. He turned quickly and I saw his hand go to his pistol and then, Merida shook his head, smiled and continued toward his car.

As Fireball sped around the curves, I slid back and forth across the back seat. Ever so often, I thought I could hear the sound of jars clicking against each other but, didn't think much about it. "Probably just some old empty pop bottles in the trunk." I reasoned with myself.

We saw a couple of deputy sheriff cars along the way but they only waved at us as we sped along. Soon we had crossed the county line into Madison County and arrived in Richmond. Fireball took us to the Union Bus Station and came to a stop.

"Here we are Willie. Safe and sound. I don't see that Black Brother's bus anywhere around so we must have beat them. You go on inside and wait for Ethel Mae. I have to go up the street here for a few minutes."

"Bless you, Fireball." Willie said. "Now don't you go off and leave me here 'cause me and Ethel Mae will need you to take us back home. " Then Willie looked at me sitting in the back seat. "What about Dank? Is he going with you or staying with me."

"Ah, he can go with me or stay with you either one. It's whatever he wants' to do." Fireball said.

"I'm going to go with Willie. I ain't never been in a big city bus station before," I answered as Willie held up the passenger seat and allowed me to climb out of the car.

Willie and I entered the bus station as Fireball slowly drove away. As we walked inside, I saw the long seats with people sitting on them and a counter where a man stood selling bus tickets. Willie and I approached the man and Willie asked, "What time does the Black Brothers Bus from Booneville get here and what time does the Greyhound bus for Dayton, Ohio leave here?" Willie asked.

The man smiled and said, "Son, I'm going to have to answer your questions one at a time because the answer to both ain't the same answer. Black Brothers will be here in exactly 12 minutes and the bus to Dayton leaves in exactly 33 minutes."

"Thank you kindly, Sir." Willie said.

Willie looked at me and pointing toward the long benches in the waiting room said, "Well, we might as well sit down and wait, I guess."

Willie and I sat down. I looked around and saw a boy about my age sitting next to me. He was dressed in a blue suit with a white shirt and tie and black dress shoes. I noticed him looking at me.

"Howdy." I said.

The boy didn't answer me but continued to stare at my cut off blue jeans and bare feet. I wasn't wearing a shirt.

"My name's Dank." I said.

The boy still did not answer. I saw the woman sitting next to him look at me and then, turning her nose upward, she quickly looked away.

As I was attempting to strike up a conversation with the boy, Willie stood and walked to the door of the Bus Station.

"My name is Dank." I repeated. "Have you got a name?" And again, the boy did not answer but just stared at me.

I shrugged my shoulders and looked around the large room. I noticed Willie open the door of the bus station and walk outside. I stood and followed. I saw why Willie had left in such a rush. The long limousine style Black Brothers bus had pulled into the station and Willie was watching it closely. I sat down on the street curb and watched Willie as he shifted his weight from one foot to the other. I saw him smile and I looked into the direction he was gazing and saw Ethel Mae climbing out of the bus.

Ethel Mae was wearing a blue skirt and white blouse and her long black hair glistened in the bright sunlight. She stood, waiting for the driver to retrieve her luggage and then turned to walk toward the station. She saw Willie standing in front of her and I saw a smile come to her lips.

"Why Willie Green, what in the world are you doing in Richmond? Are you leaving Owsley County too?" she asked.

"No Ethel Mae, I came all the way down here to see you. I just heard a little while ago that you was leaving the county and I just had to get down here as fast as I could. I need to talk to you Ethel Mae, if you don't mind and I got something real important to ask you."

Well, the driver told me the Greyhound bus would be leaving in about ten minutes or so… I guess I have a few minutes before I would have to leave."

"Thank you, Ethel Mae. Here, let me take that suitcase." Willie said as he reached to take the cardboard suitcase from Ethel Mae's hand and then continued. "Maybe we can step right over here a little ways. That is if you don't want to sit down."

"Yes, Willie… Over there would be fine. I think I will be sitting for quite a while and it will be good to stand for a little bit." Ethel answered.

I watched as Ethel Mae and Willie walked a short distance from where I sat. I saw Willie reach into his pocket and pull out the small diamond ring I had retrieved a little earlier from the creek. I saw Ethel Mae look at the ring and then at Willie. I saw Willie drop to his knee and then gaze up into the face of Ethel Mae and say something to her. I then saw Ethel Mae put her small hand to her mouth as tears came into her eyes. I watched as she nodded her head "yes" and then Willie stood and placed his arms around her small waist and lifted her off the ground and turned around and around. I heard Willie say in a shout, "Ethel Mae, I am the happiest man on the face of this whole big world!" And then, I heard Ethel Mae laughingly say, "Willie, put me down. You're making me dizzy." I saw Willy take Ethel Mae's small hand and place the ring on her finger.

The couple laughed and Ethel Mae held out her hand, admiring her new ring. "Oh, Willie!" she said, "It's about the prettiest thing I ever seen in all my born days."

Together, hand in hand, with Willie carrying the small suitcase they approached me.

"Dank, you get to be the very first to congratulate Ethel Mae and me on our soon to be wedding."

I stood, shook hands with Willie and then said, "Congratulations to both of you." Ethel Mae wrapped her arms around me, my face buried in her stomach, and said, "Oh, Dank…. I am the happiest girl in this country."

"We're going back to Owsley County together." Willie said. Then he stopped, looked around quickly and continued "Now where in the world is that Fireball. I'll bet you that skunk has left us here. It's no telling what he's off doing."

About that time I heard the familiar sound of Fireball's 1951 Ford that he lovingly called "Black Thunder" come to a screeching stop at the bus station.

"There he is, Willie." I said.

"Good." Willie said with a sound of relief. "Let's go Ethel Mae. You and me can ride in the back seat on the way back home.

"Wait Willie," Ethel Mae interrupted. "I need to get a refund on my bus ticket. Money is money and I think we're going to need it bad if we set up housekeeping."

You're right," Willie agreed. "Come on."

Fireball had gotten out of his car and was walking toward us when Willie said, "Fireball, we'll be right back. If you don't care, put Ethel Mae's suitcase in your trunk. We're going into the bus station and get her ticket money back and then we'll be ready to go."

"Sounds good to me." Fireball replied, taking the suitcase from Willie's outstretched hand.

Fireball and I walked to the car but, instead of putting the suitcase into the trunk, he laid it on the front seat between him and myself. "Ain't no need to put this little thing in that big trunk, Dank." Fireball reasoned. I shrugged my shoulders as if it didn't matter to me, one way or the other.

Soon Willie and Ethel Mae returned to the car, climbed into the back seat, and Fireball slowly drove through the streets of Richmond heading in the direction of Booneville. Just as we approached the Madison and Estill County line, I heard a siren and turned to look though the back window. I saw a Deputy Sheriff's car behind us with his blue light flashing.

"You weren't going too fast were you Fireball?" Willie asked.

"Nope… going under the speed limit and staying on my side of the road." Fireball responded.

I watched as a short, bald man climbed out of the Deputy's car. He was wearing a pair of blue jeans and brown shirt with a badge on the chest. He had a gun belt and holster around his waist and his hand rested on the gun as he walked slowly toward the driver's side.

He came to the driver's window and peered inside. "Well, ain't this my lucky day." he said. "Fireball Goosey, is that really you. Why boy, you are a legend in these parts. Don't recon you got any shine in that trunk of yours do you? Better not lie to me now, boy."

Fireball smiled and looked at the deputy. "Well sir, I'm going to let you be the judge of that. As a matter of fact, I'm down this way on a mission of mercy. I brought one of the sickest men I ever saw in my life all the way from Owsley County to Richmond. He was lovesick and had been shot right through the heart with Cupid's arrow. Why, ain't no doubt about it, Deputy, that man would have died just as sure as my name is Fireball Goosey if I hadn't got him down this way when I did."

Willie chimed in from the backseat, "That's the gospel truth! It sure is Deputy. And, I'm the man he's talking about. I was about as sick as a man could get. I was sicker than when I ate all them June apples out of my Granddaddies apple orchard when I was ten years old. I had more pain in this body than when I got that nest of hornets riled and they stung me thirty-seven times before I could get away from them. But right now, I'm cured and it's all because of Fireball being so good in bringing me down here to catch my sweet Ethel Mae before she left this state forever. This is her sitting right next to me."

Ethel Mae smiled at the Deputy and waved her small hand.

"So you're the one we got that call about," the deputy said. "Some Constable in Owsley County called and said somebody was burning the roads up on a mission of love and asked that we just turn our heads the other way if they passed by."

"Yes Sir, it was me," Fireball answered as he smiled and hit the steering wheel of his car.

"Well, all right!" the deputy said. "You can be on your way but listen to me good. You better keep that supped up car of yours under the speed limit if you know what's good for you…. I'll let the fellows over in Estill and Lee know that you've already been checked so they won't have to waste their time on you."

"Thank you kindly, Deputy," Fireball said "And yes sir, I will stay well under the speed limit."

The Deputy turned and walked back to his car as Fireball slowly pulled back onto the highway and we began our journey home.

The trip took about an hour and I could hear Willie and Ethel Mae talking in the back seat, even though Fireball had his radio turned up loud and was singing along with the songs. I think he knew about every word to every song on the radio. A few times I looked into the back seat and saw Willie and Ethel Mae holding hands and staring at each other and laughing together.

"Dank," Fireball said "I should have been a singer. Don't you think I'm a good singer? I might just pack up and head off to Nashville one of these days and try my hand at that singing. I believe I could do as well as old Carl Perkins or Johnny Cash or even that Elvis fellow everyone seems crazy about."

"I think you'd do real good, Fireball," I answered.

After arriving in Owsley County, Fireball looked into his rear-view mirror, turned the radio down and said, "Well, where do you want me to drop you two love birds off at?"

"Take us to Ethel Mae's house." Willie said. "We got a lot of plans to make."

"Yes!" Ethel Mae agreed. "Take us to my house and I want to see the look on Momma and Daddy"s face when we get out of the car. Momma bawled her eyes out when I left home this morning and Daddy was so sad he couldn't hardly talk to me without big tears coming into his eyes."

"Then that's where we're going." Fireball said.

We turned into the hollow where Ethel Mae lived and drove about a mile to the small four room frame house that was her home. Ethel Mae's mother and father, along with her younger four sisters and two brothers came from behind the house and watched as Ethel Mae climbed from the back seat, accompanied by Willie and walked toward them. The brothers and sisters shouted and came running to greet Ethel Mae, grabbing her around the legs and pulling at her arms. I saw Ethel Mae's mother take a small handkerchief from her apron pocket and wipe her eyes as a smile came to her lips. I saw Ethel Mae's father, a short and stocky man with overalls shake his head and smile broadly.

"Hey Willie," Fireball called after the couple. "Don't forget this suit case."

Willie turned and came back to the car, took the suit case from Fireball and said, "Fireball, you don't know how much I appreciate this. You are a true friend and I want you to be the best man at our wedding. There wouldn't have been a wedding if you hadn't helped me like you did."

"Even though I tried to kill you this morning?" Fireball smiled.

"Yep, and I guess I'm glad for even that." Willie responded. "If you hadn't almost killed me you wouldn't have been beholden to me enough to take me all the way to Richmond."

Fireball nodded his head and walked back to the car as I followed close behind.

"Guess you want me to take you back to the store, don't you Dank?" Fireball said.

"Yep, that'll be good." I answered.

"I need to make one quick stop first, Dank. Won't take very long at all." Fireball said.

We rode in silence as Fireball took a turn to Duck Fork and drove to the home of Squeeky Mays. Squeeky was the biggest bootlegger in this part of the county and everybody knew it. "Now don't you tell anybody we came here!" Fireball cautioned.

"I won't tell anybody." I promised.

Fireball pulled behind the house and tooted his horn. Squeeky came onto the back porch and stepped down onto the ground, walking quickly to the car. Fireball opened his door and stepped outside. "Now you stay in the car, Dank." Fireball again ordered. I nodded my head yes.

Fireball opened his trunk and I watched as he and Squeeky unloaded cases of Pabst Blue Ribbon Beer from the trunk, stacking it onto the back porch. I then saw Squeeky reach into his pocket and pull out a wad of money and began counting it, placing it carefully into Fireball's outstretched hand.

"Thank you kindly, Squeeky." Fireball said as he shook hands with Squeeky and then returned to the car.

I saw a broad smile on Fireball's face as he looked at me, turned on his radio and began to sing *"Well, you can burn my house, you can steal my car, drink my liquor from an old fruit jar, do anything that you wanna do but uh uh honey lay off of my shoes and don't you, step on my blue suede shoes. Well, you can do anything but lay off of my blue suede shoes"*

As we pulled up in the front of the store, Fireball looked at me and said, "Dank, it's an amazing thing to me how much beer city folks will trade for just a little bit of moonshine."

After the car stopped, I opened the door and got out, quickly moving out of the way as Fireball sped off, flinging gravels and dust and singing at the top of his voice. *"Well, you can knock me down, step on my face Slander my name all over the place And do anything that you want to do But uh uh honey lay off of my shoes And don't you step on my blue suede shoes You can do anything but lay off of my blue suede shoes."*

Chapter 6

The Prophet

It was on a Friday night late in July of my tenth year. All the neighbors had gathered at our home and were sitting in lawn chairs in our front yard. This was a weekly ritual for our neighbors, and they would alternate between homes during the summer. Arthur and Daisy, Gentry and Nora, Robert and Hazel along with my mother and father would sit for hours discussing the events of the week and the conversations would always run the gamut of local, state and national politics, crops, weather, and the latest gossip that was circulating.

I lay on the cool ground and listened as each took their turn in offering observations about each subject. Minnie Pearl, my Beagle Hound and constant companion lay next to me, snuggled close to my side. I was amazed at the knowledge each held of families within the county. Not only did they know the families by name and age, but they knew each family member, their parents, grandparents, aunts, uncles, cousins and all their failures and virtues.

As the adults were talking, Robert, a cousin to my mother and an auctioneer by trade, asked, "Have you all seen the Prophet yet?"

Arthur spoke in his unique language of times long past, "No, but I've sure heard a lot about him. My brother, Oak, was walking his property line a few weeks ago over at Endee and he saw this fellow dressed in a long white robe just sitting there in the woods on an old hickory log. It scared Oak half to death. Probably a good thing that Oak didn't see him twice." Arthur laughed and continued. "Oak said he was just sitting there, had his arms up in the air and was looking up into the trees. Wouldn't saying a word, Just sitting all still like he was in a trance or something."

"I recon he's been seen all over the county," Gentry added. "My brother Finley was out in his fields looking for his milk cow and saw this white robed fellow just walking around in his pasture, nodding his head back and forth. He had long black hair and was skinny as a rail. Zeke Moore saw him when he was squirrel hunting and said his long white beard reached to his belly button and his hair reached all the way down to his tail bone. Claude Smith saw him when he was cutting locusts to make some fence posts and swears that his hair and beard was a red as strawberries in the summer. Seems like everyone that sees him always see something different. It might be their eyes are just seeing what their mind tells them they ought to see."

"You know who he is, don't you?" Nora asked as everyone turned to look at her. Nora smiled and said, "Why he's Wallace Wilson, son of Joe Wilson and Bertha. They lived over near Big Sturgeon. Martin Wilson was his Granddaddy on his Daddy's side and Millard Mainous was his Granddaddy on his mother's side."

"I thought that boy died when he was just a little sprout…. Got drowned in the creek below their house." Momma said.

Nora shook her head and answered, "No, they had this boy not long after that and they kept him real close. His momma never would let him out of her sight. They wouldn't even send him to school… she did the schooling herself right in her home. I don't think they would even let that boy walk to the outhouse or do anything without one of them was with him. Don't think they got him off that place very often. I don't really know anybody that has ever seen the child. Seems like after the death of that other little boy and the birthing of this one, Joe and Bertha just kept to themselves… Never visited anyone or had anyone to visit with them. You remember, Bertha died about four or five months ago. Just had a few family members and the burial service right there at their home. Bless their hearts, Joe and that boy are just making do by themselves."

As the sun began to set, the neighbors each said their good-byes and returned to their homes. Momma, Daddy and I went inside and got ready for bed. That night, as I lay in my small upstairs bedroom, I thought about the Prophet and wondered what he looked like. "Sure would like to see him sometime," As I drifted off to sleep I thought to myself, "I've heard the preacher talk about Prophets but I ain't never seen one for myself."

I climbed out of bed early the next morning, dressed and after completing my chores, went to the smoke house to gather my fishing pole and tackle box. I was supposed to meet Jackie Dooley, a school friend and neighbor, at his home for a day of fishing at a farm lake near his home.

Jackie was my best friend. He was smaller than me but we were the same age. He had thick red hair and freckles and was built like a little bull dog. During the summers we were close companions, hunting, fishing, and playing together almost every day.

I left home with my fishing gear and made my way to Jackie's home. He lived about a mile from me up a dirt road that intersected with other roads some distance away. I hadn't travelled very far along the narrow stretch of road until I heard someone yell at me. "Hey, Dank! Where you going so bright and early this morning?"

I stopped and turned to the sound of the voice. I saw Billy Boy Margraves sitting on the bank above the road, leaned against an oak tree. He held a quart Mason jar in one hand and a cigarette in the other. A train engineer's cap set slantingly on his head and he wore railroad style overalls (though he had never worked on the railroad) brogans, and a checked flannel shirt.

Billy Boy was about sixty years old. I had wondered why everyone called him Billy Boy and Dad once told me that Billy Boy's father was also named Billy and, from the time of his birth people had always called him Billy Boy to differentiate between the two. Billy Boy had never married and still lived with his father and mother, both now into their eighties. He worked each day with his father on the farm and sometimes hired himself out to help other people during the hay and tobacco seasons.

I held my fishing pole up and said, "Me and Jackie Dooley are going fishing up at the lake."

"I should have knowed that by the looks of things, being as observant as I am." Billy Boy said. "Boy, Dank, I sure do wish that I could get a little time to go fishing." Then, taking a drink from the Mason jar, Billy Boy continued, "I can't get time to do nothing at all since I got that new job with the county."

"What new job?" I asked

"Hush your mouth, Boy!" Billy Boy screamed. "You mean you ain't heard about my new job. Why, I thought everybody in the county knowed about that job by now! It's probably the most important job anybody in this county ever had and the County Judge and Magistrates picked me specially to get that job done."

"What do you do?" I asked

Well, Sir, I'll tell you," Billy Boy said as he took a long draw from his cigarette and blew the smoke into the cool morning air. "I got to patrol the whole border of this county and keep all the elephants run off… Heaven only knows what would happen if them elephants ever got into Owsley County and tore up people's crops and knocked down their barns and run wild amongst the children and women folks. That would be the most awful sight anybody ever seen. Yes sir, it's the most important job anybody ever had."

"I ain't never seen no elephants nowhere near this county, Billy Boy." I said.

"Well praise the Lord, Dank. I'm glad to hear that. Guess it means I'm doing an awful good job then, don't you think?" and then Billy Boy took another drink from his Mason Jar, slapped his knee and laughed.

I shook my head, turned and started walking back up the road and behind me I heard Billy Boy yell, "Now Dank, you be on the look-out for me and if you should happen to see a elephant anywhere near this county, you come running and let me know just as quick as your legs will carry you." I could hear his loud laughter as I walked out of his sight.

"He's a crazy old man," I thought to myself as I quickened my pace.

As I neared Jackie's house, I saw him sitting on the front porch.

Jackie lived in a large, two story frame farm house, surrounded by pastures and barns. It was on the top of a steep knoll and a portion of the home had originally been a log house. When you entered the living room you could see the logs that were still unfinished on the inside walls, as was a kitchen and two bedrooms.

"I thought you was never in the world going to get here!" Jackie yelled as I started up the knoll toward the porch. Before I could reach the porch, Jackie continued, "I got big news, Dank. They's been a gas leak down near Ida Mae and Daddy's got to go and walk the gas line. He's going to take us down to Big Sturgeon Creek and we can fish all morning." Jackie's father worked for the gas line company and it was his job to walk their lines and, periodically, blow the gas valves to keep moisture out of the lines.

I ran up the remainder of the hill and then sat down on the porch next to Jackie.

"Momma's got us some biscuit sandwiches of ham and jelly to take with us," Jackie continued holding up a small brown bag containing our lunch. "They's a store close by and Daddy's gonna stop and buy each of us a pop. This is going to be the most wonderful day of the summer, Dank. Lots of good fishing in that Big Sturgeon Creek." Jackie declared.

"That sounds mighty fine to me. First time I ever got to go down there to fish." I replied.

Jackie's father, Conley, came onto the porch and said, "Well, you boys ready to go?" I turned and saw Conley dressed in his work clothes with high top boots for protection against the rattlesnakes and copperheads that infested the woods. He wore a pistol in a holster on his hip and carried a large knife in his hand for cutting brush near the gas lines.

"Yes sireee Bob we're ready." Jackie said as we both stood and walked with Conley to his old green pick-up truck. We placed our fishing gear and small paper bag containing our delicacies in the back of the truck along with Conley's large knife and then climbed into the cab. Conley started the engine and we were on our way to the mouth of Big Sturgeon.

As we drove down the dirt road to the main highway, I saw Billy Boy Margraves lying under the Oak tree where I had seen him sitting.

"I want you to look at that." Conley said, "That looks like Billy Boy Margraves laying there. I hope he ain't dead." He came to a screeching stop, flinging Jackie and me against the dashboard of the truck.

Conley got out of the truck and rushed over to where Billy Boy lay. I saw him pick up the Mason jar, smell of it, and then throw it down and return to the truck, shaking his head back and forth. When he climbed into the truck, Jackie asked, "Was he dead?"

"Yep, son, he surely is….. He's dead drunk." Conley answered.

Once again, we continued our journey to the best fishing hole in the area. As we sped through Ida Mae, just before we reached the Heidelberg Bridge that spanned the Kentucky River, Conley turned off the road and onto a small dirt path that led to the creek. After he came to a stop on the shoal that bordered the creek, Jackie and I quickly jumped from the truck grabbing our fishing gear from the bed of the truck. Conley, still sitting behind the wheel said, "Now boys, you be careful," and then reaching into his pocket he pulled out two quarters. "Here," he said, handing the money to Jackie. "In case you want to get some pops or other sandwiches or something, just go down the creek a little piece and you'll find a path that leads up to the bridge. Go over to Updyke's grocery just on the other side of the river and get whatever you want. It's going to take me about four hours or so to walk the gas line, but I'll be by to pick you up right after I finish."

"All right, Daddy." Jackie answered. "Just you watch out for rattlesnakes and don't you get bit or nothing.

Conley then backed the truck up and turned sharply around. After he reached the highway, I could hear the sound of the engine as Conley changed gears and sped away.

"This is sure going to be a good day," Jackie said "and look what I got here in my pocket." He reached into his back pocket and pulled out a plug of Days Work chewing tobacco. "I slipped this out of daddy's room before we left this morning." Then, reaching into his front pocket he pulled out a Barlow knife and cut a thin sliver off the moist plug of tobacco. "Here, Dank," he said as he handed it to me. "This is the best chew you will ever have."

I took the sliver of tobacco and placed it into my jaw. It was not the first chew of tobacco I had ever had but it was usually store-bought Apple. That was the brand of choice of my uncles or homegrown twists that they made and slipped to me when my parents weren't watching.

The Days Work tasted good and I watched as Jackie cut another small slice from the plug and placed it into his jaw.

"Now, let's catch us some fish." Jackie said. We busily prepared our hooks for the water and hoped that the mouth of a waiting bass or catfish that lurked under the water would find the fat, juicy worms so tempting they couldn't resist a free meal.

I finished baiting my hook before Jackie had finished baiting his and started to throw my baited hook into the creek. Wait!" Jackie yelled. "Wait! We ain't done our good luck thing yet."

"I forgot... Guess I was just too excited." I said.

Jackie laughed and joined me as we stood at the edge of the creek and then spat a thin spray of amber juice into the clear stream. "That ought to make the fish sit up and take notice." Jackie said as I nodded my head in agreement.

After our hooks had been cast into the water, we sat down on the sandy shoal and waited for the first tug on the lines. An hour passed and we still hadn't gotten any bites. We lay on the rocky bank of the creek and gazed into the clear blue sky. We talked about all those things important to ten-year-old boys.... dogs, fishing, hunting, school, girls and what we wanted most for Christmas. I heard the rustling of the paper bag and turned to see Jackie pulling out a large biscuit and jelly sandwich. "Want one, Dank?" he asked. "Nope, not right now." I answered.

I stood and walked to the edge of the creek. My eyes turned to the opposite bank and I saw a man in a long white robe with a rope belt around his waist. He was looking at me and I could see that his hair was as white as fresh fallen snow and he appeared to be a boy in a man's body. Slowly I raised my hand and waved at him. He waved back to me. "So that's what a real to life Prophet looks like!" I thought to myself. "Why, he ain't no different than most folk 'cept for that big old robe he's wearing."

We stared at each other for several minutes when Jackie yelled.... "I've got a big one. Dank. I believe he's the biggest fish in this whole creek." I turned to see Jackie with his fishing pole in his hands and he was slowly reeling in the fish. I walked to where Jackie stood and waited to see the fish he had caught. I saw remnants of the strawberry jelly around Jackie's lips and he clenched his teeth and continued to reel in the fish. As it came near to the shore, I saw the fish rise out of the water, twist and then, the line went limp. "Durn it!" Jackie screamed. "He done got away. I swear Dank that would have been the prize fish in this whole county if I could have got it on this bank."

I turned my gaze once again to the opposite side of the creek and the Prophet had disappeared. I looked up and down the creek but didn't see him. I looked into the tree line above the creek and he wasn't there either. I wondered to myself, "Where has he gone?"

After Jackie baited his hook and threw his line back into the creek, he turned to me and said, "Let's go down to the store and get us a Nehi orange pop, Dank. I sure do like those big old orange drinks, and if we got enough money, we'll get us a baloney sandwich. I ain't really in the mood for ham and biscuits when you can eat a slice of baloney."

"Sounds like a good idea to me." I answered. We walked along the edge of the creek to the small path that led to the bridge across the Kentucky River. As we walked across the bridge we would stop and stare over the sides at the greenish water of the river. "Bet there's all kinds of big ole catfish in that River, Dank! Wish we had us a boat! We'd get right out in the middle of that thing and fish ourselves to death."

We walked to the store that set at the end of the bridge. It was an old metal building with benches on the front porch. Two old men were sitting on one of the benches, whittling and chewing tobacco. "Yes sir, as the Lord is my witness, I just saw that Prophet right on the other side of the river there." I heard one of the men say.

"They ain't no sich a thing as Prophets in this country." the other man chided. "Them prophet fellers were all over there in that place where them Jews live. Why, the Good Lord wouldn't allow no Prophets to come around here. That would be against the Bible."

"Well, say whatever you want,! I know what I seen!" The first man answered. "Why he was standing there as bright as day, on the other side of the river just looking down there at the Creek and then he raised up his hand and did some kind of strange motion. Then he just up and walked away, right up there into them trees on that hill over there. If the Good Lord wanted to send one of them Prophets into this country, I guess He could do it! Wouldn't be nothing to stop Him if He took a notion to."

Jackie and I entered the store. It was dark and a man stood leaned over the counter writing in some small account books. He looked up and smiled. "What can I do for you two young saplins?" he asked.

"We're going to get us some Nehi orange pops." Jackie answered.

"Right there in the back, in the pop cooler." the man said, pointing to the rear of the store.

We walked to the cooler, got our pops and returned to the counter to pay.

"Do you want a sandwich?" Jackie asked. We got enough money for a good baloney sandwich and we'll save the ham until later."

"Sure." I replied. "I think I'll have a baloney sandwich."

"Me too," Jackie responded. "We'll each have us a big baloney sandwich, sir." Jackie told the man.

I watched as the man took a large roll of bologna and then with a large butcher knife cut two thick slices of meat, and returned to the counter. He opened a loaf of Kerns Bread and then placed each of the slices of meat between the bread making a sandwich for each of us.

"Want some onions?" He asked, "Or have you two young bucks got some girls fishing with you over on the creek?" and then laughed.

"Nah!" Jackie responded. "It's just us. Yeah, I want a piece of onion and a slice of tomato too." Jackie said.

"Me too" I said.

The man placed onions and tomatoes on the sandwiches and then wrapped them in wax paper before placing them into a small brown bag. As he worked on the sandwiches, he asked "Are you two young sprouts going to be doing any swimming while you're at the creek?"

Don't know," I answered, "Hadn't thought about that."

"Do both of you know how to swim?" He asked.

"Sure." Jackie and I responded simultaneously.

"Good." he continued and then asked, "Who taught you how to swim?"

"My daddy taught me." I answered.

"My daddy taught me, too." Jackie echoed.

"That's good," The man said as he continued to prepare the sandwiches. "Dads are the best to teach you how to swim. My dad taught me right over there in that river. I probably was just a few months past being five years old when he took me over to the river and just threw me in."

Jackie and I stared at each other and then at the man behind the counter.

"I took to swimming just like a fish," He said. "Wouldn't nothing hard about it at all."

He paused and then continued, "I guess for me the hardest thing was getting out of the sack my daddy had put me in."

I looked at Jackie and his mouth was wide open and his eyes were as large as saucers. "How did you get out of the sack?" Jackie asked.

The man looked at Jackie with a surprised expression on his face as though Jackie should have known the answer to the question. "You mean you don't know how to get out of a sack?" he said. And then moving his head back and forth he continued, "Why it's the simplest thing on earth. You just turn the sack inside out." I noticed the corner of his mouth turn up slightly as though he was fighting back a smile.

"Here we are, fellows." he said. "Now, let's see here. Two sandwiches and two Nehi pops. That'll be thirty-five cents."

Jackie reached into his pocket and pulled out two quarters. He received his change and we left the store. The two old men were still arguing about the Prophet as Jackie and I made our way across the bridge and back down the small path to the bank of the creek.

As we got to the creek bank, I saw the Prophet standing on the opposite side of the creek where our poles were. Jackie saw him at the same time as I did, and we stopped in our tracks. "Oh, Lord have mercy! It's an angel!" Jackie said. "I've seen pictures of them in Momma's big old Bible. Oh, Dear Lord! What have we done to make the Good Lord send an angel to get us?"

"That ain't no angel." I responded.

"Maybe you're right." Jackie answered. "He don't have none of them wings on his back like I seen in the picture. He must be one of them saints that the Bible is always talking about. Oh, Dank!, What have we done to make the Good Lord send a Saint down here to see us right on the best day of our life?"

"That's no Saint, Jackie," I disagreed. "That's The Prophet people are talking about. I saw him earlier over on the other side of the creek. He won't hurt us. He even waved at me a while ago."

"Oh, dear Lord!" Jackie sobbed. "That's even worse. Prophets always come to bring curses and damnation on people.…. I don't want to be yelled at or cursed by no Prophet. They can make big balls of fire come flying down out of the sky and burn people to smithereens. I don't even know what I've done to deserve being yelled at or burnt to a crisp like a slice of jowl bacon. I did put a little bit of green dye in my sister's shampoo bottle, but it didn't really hurt her none except give her some green hair for a few days. And then I did sneak that plug of chewing tobacco out of Daddy's bedroom. But that's no sin, is it Dank?"

"I don't think it is." I answered while keeping my eyes on the Prophet. Once more I waved at him. He slowly raised his hand and waved back.

Jackie and I continued to walk to our fishing poles as the Prophet measured our slow, cautious progress.

When we reached the poles the Prophet began to walk up the creek for several yards, stopped and then turned to face the creek. He slowly stepped off the bank and began to walk across the creek, as though he was walking on the water.

Jackie fell down on his knees and began to sobbingly pray, "Oh, dear Lord. Whatever I've done to make you so mad at me that you would send a real to goodness Prophet to set me straight, forgive me right now and here! Don't let that Prophet turn me into a toad frog or burn me to a crisp or give me boils on my body!"

I continued to watch the Prophet as he made his way across the creek and then he turned to face Jackie and me. He raised his right hand and then waved his hand back and forth.

I raised my hand and also waved. I had never met a Prophet before. I guess the closest thing to a Prophet I had ever met was a preacher who had come into the county some years earlier. He wore a white suit and was able to heal people right on the spot no matter what their ailment. Some said that he had even made crippled people throw their crutches away and they could leap and dance just like they had never had anything wrong with them.

The Prophet began to walk toward us. I turned and saw Jackie still kneeling but now he had buried his face into the rocky creek bank.

"Get up Jackie! I commanded. "He's walking toward us."

"No Dank." Jackie whimpered. "I can't. That Prophet has paralyzed me. I can't raise up or stand or nothing. Besides all that I think I might have peed on myself."

"He's done no such thing!" I said. "You're acting like a little girl. If you don't get up right now!, I'm never going hunting or fishing or swimming with you ever again. Now get up on your feet and act like a man." I scolded.

Slowly Jackie raised up and then stood, walking carefully next to where I stood. He got so close to me that a stranger would have thought we must be Siamese Twins.

The Prophet walked to where we stood and for the first time I could see his face. He had slightly slanted eyes, a small chin and a short neck.

I had seen another person who had looked pretty much like the Prophet in Booneville some time earlier. He was a grown man, but he talked like a kid and his speech was somewhat slurred. When I had asked dad about him, he had said that the man was a "gifted" or a "special" creation of God. His name was Campbell and he was twenty-seven years old and lived with his parents.

"Have you caught any fish?" the Prophet asked.

"Nope." I answered. "But we expect to catch a lot."

The Prophet sat down on the rocky creek bank and stared out into the creek.

"You're in the wrong spot. Go about twenty steps down the creek and try again." He said.

Jackie and I took our fishing poles and cast our lines out into the creek to the spot the Prophet suggested.

We had no more than cast our baited hooks out into the creek before we each got bites and snagged two good bass.

As we placed the fish onto the stringer, I looked at the Prophet still sitting in the same spot watching our actions and smiling. We rebaited our hooks and cast out our lines a second time in the same spot. No sooner had they settled to the bottom of the creek than we each caught a catfish. Once again, we repeated our actions from before, stringing the fish, rebaiting our hooks and casting our lines into the creek. For a third time we each caught fish and, in our excitement we had forgotten the Prophet.

After about fifteen minutes of fishing with such success the fish suddenly stopped biting. It was at that time we noticed that the Prophet had suddenly disappeared.

"Where did he go?" Jackie asked. I shrugged my shoulders.

"He had to be a Prophet, Dank!" Jackie said. "He knew right where them old fish was a hiding and waiting. Kinda like what I learned one Sunday in Sunday school. Jesus told His disciples' right where they should be fishing, and they caught a whole boat full of fish. Just wait 'til I tell Daddy what just happened."

I scanned the opposite bank of the creek and then the hillside. I looked up and down the creek on our side. I ran down to where the Sturgeon emptied into the Kentucky River and looked in both directions, but the Prophet was gone.

When I returned Jackie was carefully examining the stringer full of bass and catfish.

"I didn't see him nowhere." I announced.

"He probably just took a notion to vanish. Prophets can do that if they want to." Jackie said. "All they have to do is just think of themselves being in another place and *poof,* they are just there. Anyways, didn't you see him walking on the water when he came across that creek? If he can do that it wouldn't be nothing for him to just up and vanish if he wanted to."

I heard the sound of a truck engine behind me. I turned and saw Jackie's father arriving to pick us up. He skid to a stop on the rocky shoal and got out of the truck, walking toward us.

"Well boys, let me see that mess of fish you caught." Jackie proudly lifted the stringer full of fish for him to see."

"That's a mighty fine catch of fish." Conley said. "Bring it on over here and we'll put them in the cooler in the back of the truck."

Jackie carried the string of fish, using both hands to lift them, while I retrieved our fishing poles. We placed them into the truck bed, climbed into the cab of the truck and began the journey home.

"Guess what me and Dank seen today, Daddy?" Jackie said.

"I don't rightly know, Jackie." Conley answered. "Why don't you just tell me?"

"We saw us a real to life Prophet!" Jackie exclaimed.

"A Prophet? You don't say!" Conley answered. "And where did you see this Prophet?"

"Right there on the creek bank. He was on the other side of the creek and then he walked on the water and crossed the creek and told us where we needed to throw our lines to catch the fish. Then he just disappeared into the thin air. Just ask Dank if you don't believe me" Jackie said excitedly.

"Not that I don't believe you Jackie but, is that true, Dank?"

"Yes Sir!" I answered, "It sure is and he was dressed in a long white robe and had a face that was just like the face of a little child except it was a little bit different."

"You mean you got close enough to him to see his face?" Conley asked.

"Yes" Jackie and I answered simultaneously. And then I continued, "He came right up to us and sat down on the rocks on the shoal where we was fishing. Then after telling us where to fish, he just vanished."

"Well, I'll be." Conley said.

Nothing more was said until we reached my home. Conley, Jackie and I walked to the rear of the truck to get my fishing pole. "Which of these fish is yours, Dank?" Conley asked.

"You just keep 'em." I said. "I just was glad to get to go fishing today, and I really don't like to skin catfish that much."

"Well your daddy might enjoy a mess of catfish. Don't you want to take a couple of these with you? They would make for mighty good eating." Conley said.

"No. Not today. Besides, we got some catfish stored in the freezer." I replied.

"Well, you boys will have to do this again this summer," Conley said. "I might be back down that way again in a few weeks."

Jackie and Conley got back into the truck cab and I waved at them as they sped off.

About two weeks passed from the time of our encounter with the Prophet. I had started to the barn about midmorning when I heard someone call my name. I stopped and looked around to determine where the voice was coming from.

"Hey Dank!" the voice called again. "Come on over here and help me eat some of these apples."

I saw Gentry Isaacs sitting in a green metal lawn chair in his front yard. I walked across the road and took a seat next to him.

"Well, Dank. Get one of the apples and tell me if they're any good and then tell me what adventures you have had since school let out for the summer.

I picked out a large, red, apple. Taking my Barlow pocketknife from my jean pocket I cut off a slice.

"Me and Jackie Dooley went fishing down at the mouth of Big Sturgeon a couple weeks ago and I saw the Prophet."

"Is that so?" Gentry asked.

"Yep!" I answered.

"Was he wearing that big long white robe?" Gentry asked.

"He sure was." I replied. "And he walked on water. He was on the other side of the creek and walked across it just as easy as walking on the ground."

"Where at the mouth of the creek was you fishing, Dank?" Gentry asked.

"We were on the rock shoal." I answered.

"I know that spot." Gentry said. "I've fished there lots of times. Would he, by chance, have been a few yards above the shoal when he come walking across the creek?"

I nodded my head and answered, "Yes."

"Well, I hate to be a spoilsport, Dank, but did you know there's a natural shelf divide in the creek right at that spot you're talking about. The water pools above the creek pretty deep and then it just sort of skimmers over that shelf and then pools again before it enters into the River. Chances are he knew that shelf was there and walked across on it. The creek is only about an inch or two deep in that spot at the most. I've walked to the other side of the creek on that shelf dozens of times, myself." Gentry explained.

"Well, we wasn't having much luck fishing in the spot where we was and he told us to walk down the creek several steps and then throw our fishing lines in. We caught one fish right after another when we did that." I argued.

Gentry laughed and said, "Yeah! That's about right. The big old cat fish come from the river into the mouth of the creek just about that spot. Guess that they're tired of fighting the river current and want to rest a little while in the more shallow waters of the creek. That's always a pretty good spot to fish."

We sat in silence for several minutes and then Gentry spoke again. "I don't imagine we'll be seeing any more of the Prophet around here, Dank."

"Why not?" I asked.

"Well Dank, the Prophet's daddy died some time back. Neighbors got concerned about him and his boy and went to check on them. The yard was all grown up, cows hadn't been milked or livestock fed. They found Joe dead, still laying in his bed. He had been there for several days, maybe a week or more. The boy was out in the woods just wandering around all over the place. Poor old Joe's body was in such bad shape they had to put him right into a coffin and bury him that same day."

"What about the Prophet?" I asked.

"Well, one of the neighbors took him in until some of his family came to get him. I think it was Joe's brother that lives up in Dayton or somewhere up that way. I guess he's up there with them right now."

We sat again in silence. "But at least you got to see the Prophet, Dank." Gentry said. "I guess people will be talking about him around here for a long time to come. I would say they will be talking about him a lot longer than my old bones will be on top of the ground and for a long time after they've been put under the ground."

"You recon there'll ever be another Prophet in this county, Gentry?" I asked.

"Well, I don't know, Dank." Gentry answered. "There might well be. God knows we sure do need one the way things are getting to be.

And then, taking another bite of apple, Gentry repeated, "Yes Siree, Dan! God surely knows that we need one in the worst way."

Chapter 7

Hambone

It was a warm September Saturday. Hambone Gabbard and I sat shirtless on the bank of Greasy Creek casually tossing small rocks into the shallow, crystal clear water. We enjoyed watching the confused antics of the minnows and tadpoles as they evaded the tiny missiles that disrupted their midmorning play and perhaps caused them to believe the world was coming to an end, if minnows and tadpoles have a brain large enough to think about such things.

"It don't make sense. It don't make no sense at all, Dank." Hambone said.

I looked at Hambone, his thin face covered with freckles. There were so many freckles I supposed that since there was no more room on his face for those tiny little red spots, some had slid from his face and landed onto his shoulders and arms. His skin was as pale as an autumn moon. I looked at his tangled red hair that had not been combed since the day before. Hambone was slightly taller and more than slightly thinner than me.

"A lot of things don't make sense, Hambone." I replied. "Don't make no sense to me that Marsha Moore would have a crush on something as ugly as you."

I had met Hambone on the first day of our fourth year of school at Needmore. Hambone, Jackie Dooley and I had become friends from that first day. His family had moved into our community a few weeks earlier from Buffalo Creek at the far end of the county. They had bought the Mainous place that was in the sharp bend of Gumm Holler.

"Still don't make no sense to me. Don't make no sense that you can turn a knob and see a picture of real live people on a little box no bigger than a beehive. My Daddy told me about seeing one. Last year when him and Lige Minter took our tebaccer crop to the warehouse in Lexington. Daddy walked down to the main street and went into a store just to see one of them little boxes. He said they had about 10 or 15 of them showing people dancing and singing and talking. Them people wuz no bigger than his hand. Daddy said he never thought he would ever see anything like that in all his life. They was a lot of other farmers there in their overalls and caps. They was all just shaking their heads in wonderment."

I shrugged my shoulders and continued to toss small pebbles into the creek. I listened to the sound of the creek as it murmured softly before speeding by me in its race to empty into Sturgeon Creek. I listened to the moans of the limbs of the oak and maple trees as they swayed, nudged by the unseen hand of a midmorning breeze. Within a month the green, tired leaves would turn to red, gold, orange and yellow. They would loosen their grip on the branches that nourished them and then drift downward. Some would fall on the ground and others would float aimlessly onto the flowing waters of the creek, riding the moving waters to places far beyond this place.

"Wonder where Jackie is?" I asked Hambone.

"Don't know," Hambone answered. "He said yesterday evening he would meet us here."

Hambone had spent the night with me. His parents had made the trip back to their old farm the day before to tend their tobacco crop and gather some beans, corn, tomatoes and other vegetables from their garden. They were going to spend the night there.

"I just can't get the thought out of my mind, Dank. I ain't never seen nothing like that in my whole life. In our old house we had a battery radio and we would always listen to the Grand Ole Opry on Saturday night. We didn't have no electric lights in our old house. The RECC people didn't stretch any wires for electric up where we lived in the head of Baker Branch. We just used our kerosene lanterns. Daddy would let me listen to a few other things on the radio and I always thought that was something!! We had to save our batteries though. Wouldn't do to have the battery die right in the middle of the Grand Ole Opry. Now we live in a house with electric and Daddy said he was going to buy us a new electric radio when he sells the tobacco crop. He's going to buy Momma one of them electric stoves like your Momma has, Dank. I won't have to cut kindling or bring in wood for that old wood cook stove no more. Daddy said that eating the food cooked on one of them electric stoves would just take a little getting use to, but it would shore save Momma a lot of time every day. Then she would have more time to help him in the fields.

But this beats it all, Dank. Do you recon' Gene Autry and Bugs Bunny and Hoss and Little Joe and all the other little people are floating somewhere above our heads right now? Do you recon' they stay up there somewhere all the time?"

"I don't think so." I answered. I looked at Hambone and saw that he was looking into the sky. His eyes were squinted together as though he was trying to see something in the distance. His mouth was open and his face contorted in such a way as to make his thin face appear like the gaunt face of dead people I had seen before.

Hambone and I had gotten out of bed early and watched Saturday morning cartoons and Gene Autry on the television. Hambone had heard about but had never seen a television before. We were one of the few people in our community, and perhaps the county, that had one of these magical boxes. I remembered the look on Hambone's face when we turned on the television set the night before and watched Bonanza. He was hypnotized by the small figures of Pa, Hoss, Adam and Little Joe and kept moving his head from side to side.

I stood and said, "Let's go, Hambone. I ain't waiting on Jackie all day. His old lazy bones are probably still in bed."

Hambone also stood. "Are you sure? Will he get mad at us?"

"Yep, I'm sure. He knows where the store is and if he don't find us here then that's where he'll go. And you know what? I don't care if he does get mad," I answered.

When Hambone and I arrived at the store we saw several old men already sitting on the benches of the front porch. They were involved in deep discussions of politics, crops, weather and gossip. They didn't seem to notice us as we walked past them and into the store. Hambone and I each bought a pop and then returned to the front porch. Sitting on the edge of the porch and letting our legs dangle over the side Hambone and I sat silently as we listened to the men talk.

"The Good Lord is going to come soon." Pleas Bishop said. "This old world is in such a bad shape the Good Lord ain't going to put up with it much longer. One day soon I expect to hear that old trumpet sound just like a fox horn and this old body is going to be changed in the wink of an eye."

"That old body of yours needs to be changed." Dave Pierson said. "It wouldn't hurt for that old body to take a dip in the creek every now and then with a bar of lye soap to scrub the sweat and grime off of it. I'm pretty sure the Lord wouldn't mind you having a scrubbed clean body when He comes to claim you."

A black Chevrolet coup pulled into the store parking lot and I saw Gilbert Gilbert get out. He was wearing his short sleeve white shirt, dress pants, and dress shoes. He had four ink pens in his shirt pocket and his crow black hair was greased down like a young boy getting ready to go courting.

Gilbert Gilbert was a salesman for the wholesale house in Beattyville. I had often wondered why he had the same first and last name. Daddy had told me that Gilbert's father, Bill, had thought it would be a good idea to give his son the same first name as his last name. It would make it easier for people to remember who he was. Of course, Daddy had told me he thought that Gilbert's father had been celebrating his son's birth with a gallon of moonshine and when the midwife asked him the baby boy's name he mumbled Gilbert a couple of times so that is what she had written down.

Gilbert Gilbert wasn't the only one in the county with the same first and last name. There was Wilson Wilson, Price Price, Green Green, Ross Ross, Marshall Marshall and maybe a few others. I guess a lot of fathers had been celebrating the birth of their boys.

Gilbert walked up to the porch and spoke cheerfully, "Good morning fellows. Mighty fine morning, ain't it?" And then his eyes focused on Hambone. "Say, Son ain't you Wad Gabbard's boy from off Buffalo."

"Yes, Sir. I am." Hambone answered.

"I thought so. I was up at Bill Moore's store some time ago and you was there. You was doing your Hambone song and dance for them."

Hambone grinned and nodded his head.

"Fellows, you ain't never seen a show until you've seen this boy do his Hambone song and dance," Gilbert said as he walked into the store.

Dave Pierson reached into his pocket and took out a few coins. He held up a dime and said, "Son, I sure would like to see that Hambone dance. Here's a new dime that's yours if you'll do it for me."

Hambone set his pop on the floor of the porch, walked over to Dave and took the dime. He placed it into his pocket and then walked to the middle of the porch. Hambone set his left foot down and then began to sing,

Hambone, hambone where you been?
Round the world and I'm going again
What you gonna do when you come back?
Take a little walk by the railroad track

-Willie Newburn-

Hambone began to turn in a circle, his left foot planted as solid as a fence post, his right foot turning him in a circle like a merry-go-round and he slapped his right hip with his right hand like a jockey whipping a horse.

Hambone continued to dance and sing. I was hypnotized by the antics of Hambone, his uncombed hair, his freckles, his skin as pale as an autumn moon and the expression on his face as he sang to the top of his voice. It was a sight to see and hear. It wasn't his normal speaking voice that he sang with. It was a long, mournful voice that would dip and rise and then flatten with each stomp of his right foot on the weathered and amber stained oak floor of the porch.

> *I just skinned an alley cat*
> *To make my wife a Sunday hat*

As Hambone was doing his dance, Jackie Dooley came running to the store. He stood at the edge of the porch with his eyes on Hambone. A smile was on his thin lips. Conley and Gilbert had also come out of the store and were watching the show that Hambone was putting on for the men.

> *Hambone, hambone Where's your wife*
> *Out to the kitchen, cooking beans and rice*

Jackie Dooley climbed up onto the porch and sat next to me. After Hambone finished his song and dance, the men laughed and clapped. They had smiles on their faces and Ivan Tolliver laughed so hard he got strangled on his chewing tobacco. Will Bowman slapped him on the back and a cud of chewing tobacco came flying out of his mouth and onto the porch floor. Hambone faced the men, placed his right arm across his stomach and then bowed. He then came and took his seat on the edge of the porch next to me.

"I didn't know you could sing." Jackie Dooley said to Hambone.

"Oh, I've done that since I was just a little bitty thing. I would go down to Bill Moore's store and the old men there would buy me a pop or give me a chew of tobacco to get me to sing and dance for them. That's how I got the nickname of Hambone."

While we sat on the store porch, other men would arrive and after hearing the story of Hambone's song and dance, they would give him some pocket change to do his song and dance for them as well. Each time that Hambone performed he seemed to add a few more movements or facial expressions and some variations to the rhythm of the song.

"It's getting close to Dinner time." I said. "Momma told us to be home by noon so we better be going."

"Let's wait a while longer, Dank." Jackie said. "Hambone is making all kinds of money doing his song and dance. He's going to leave here rich if we stay a little while longer."

I jumped from the porch, dusted the seat of my pants and said, "No. Momma said for us to be home and I don't want to get her mad at me. You don't want her to get mad at you either, believe me. She won't let me go fishing this afternoon if I get her mad at me."

Hambone and Jackie also leaped off the porch and we began our walk home.

As we walked home we talked about school. "Miss Mosely is a mean old witch of a teacher." Jackie said.

"She sure is." Hambone agreed.

"Miss Mosely's not mean." I defended. "She's a good teacher."

"She is so mean!" Hambone responded. "On the second day of school she used her paddle on me for no reason at all. I think because I'm a new kid she just wanted to let me know that she was boss."

"You had a chew of burley in your jaw, Hambone, and you ain't supposed to chew in school," I accused.

"I did in my old school and my old teacher would sometimes give me and the other boys a chew from a store-bought plug of tobacco." Hambone defended.

Jackie said, "When Becky Moore flipped me in the ear with her finger during class, I turned and gave her a mean look and stuck my tongue out at her. Becky yelled and told Miss Mosely that I was making funny faces at her. Miss Mosely came back to my seat, took me by the ear Becky had flipped with her finger, drug me to the blackboard, drew a circle on the blackboard and made me stick my nose in it for more than an hour."

"You didn't have your nose in that circle no more than two or three minutes." I answered.

"Well, it seemed like an hour." Jackie replied. "Besides, you like Miss Moseley because she's sparking with your cousin and she likes you cause she thinks it will carry favor with your cousin. You don't ever get into trouble because you're her little pet. I think that's what we'll start calling you, Teacher's Pet Dank."

"You do and I'll bust your hide good." I said.

We walked a few more steps, Jackie looked at me and said, "Not one paddlin' will he get cause he's Dank, Dank, The Teacher's Pet." And then he began to run. I chased after him and Hambone chased after me. We ran all the way to the back door of my home and into the kitchen.

Jackie almost ran over my mother who was standing near the kitchen door. "Well, I'm sure glad to see you boys are so anxious to eat that you came running. Take a seat at the table and I'll yell for Bob." Momma said. She walked to the back door and yelled for daddy to come and eat.

After we took our seats at the table Jackie looked at me and laughed. Hambone also began to laugh with him. I squinted my eyes, made my angry face, and said, "Just keep it up. Your chickens are getting ready to come home to roost right after we eat dinner."

I had not paid a lot of attention to the food that filled our dining room table. I had not noticed the fresh green beans and corn, cornbread and chicken, fried 'taters and new onions and country ham that had been left from breakfast. I didn't notice the pickles or cold slaw, relish and beets that Momma had arranged on the clean oil cloth that covered the table. Most everything except for Daddy's pickled pig's feet and hot peppers had come from our garden.

Daddy came into the kitchen, washed his hands at the sink, and took a seat at the head of the table. "Let's ask blessing." he said, and bowing his head he prayed, "Lord, we are thankful for your love and for this bounty of food you have placed before us. We know that it is all a gift to us from You for our nourishment. Bless this food now to these bodies we pray, Amen."

We had just begun to eat when the telephone rang. Momma got up from the table and answered the phone. "Yes, he's right here." Momma said. "Bob, it's for you."

Daddy got up from the table and spoke into the phone. "This is Bob..... Say that again..... When did this happen..... Where are you right now? I'll leave the house now and be right there." And then he hung the phone up.

"I just got a Coroner call, Emma. I have to leave but you can save me a plate of food for later. Will you step outside with me for a minute before I go?"

Momma got up from the table and followed Daddy outside. She returned in just a few minutes, looked at me, Jackie and Hambone and smiled. It wasn't her normal smile. It was a nervous smile. It was a type of smile that a person gives when they are keeping a secret deep down inside but don't want you to know they have a secret.

Jackie, Hambone and I ate hurriedly and after dinner we all stood and started to leave. "Where are you going, Dank?" Momma asked.

"We may go back down to the store but probably will go down to the creek fishing." I answered.

"I want you boys to stay right here on this farm until your Daddy gets back from his Coroner call, Dank."

"We'll be safe, Momma and we won't get into no trouble at the store or the creek." I insisted.

"Dank, I said you don't step foot off this place until your Daddy gets home and that is final." Momma commanded with a stern, authoritative look in her eyes and a firm tone to her voice.

"Yes Mam." I said meekly.

Hambone, Jackie and I left the house and went into the front yard. "What do you all want to do?" I asked.

"Maybe we could watch some more television." Hambone replied.

"Let's go into the woods and find us a good grapevine to make us a swing with." Jackie volunteered. "Or, we could shoot some basketball in the barn lot."

"Let's do that." I said.

As we walked to the barn lot a green pick-up pulled into our drive and came to a stop.

"That's my Pappy's truck!" Hambone yelled and ran to the truck. Jackie and I followed behind. I saw Hambone's mother get out of the passenger's side of the truck. She was a slim, tall woman. She was dressed in men's pants and shirt and had work boots on her feet. She had long red hair that had been pulled back into a ponytail. She had freckles on her pale face, though not as many as Hambone had on his. Hambone's Pappy also got out of the truck. He was a tall man with brown hair and shovel size hands. He looked awfully familiar, but I couldn't remember where I had seen him.

"There's my boy. There's my little man." Hambone's mother said as she hugged him. "You wait here, honey. I need to speak with Dank's mommy for just a minute." She then turned to walk toward the house. I watched her as she went to the back door and knocked. When Momma came to the door, I saw the two women hug and they disappeared into the house.

Hambone's grandfather walked to where Hambone stood and placed his large hand on Hambone's uncombed hair. "You ain't got a nest of birds in there somewhere do you Hambone?" he said as he laughed a nervous, strained laugh while rubbing Hambone's head.

"No!" Hambone answered, as though he was offended by the question, but his smile let me know that he wasn't.

"Why don't you introduce me to these two young saplings here, Hambone?"

"Sure!" Hambone replied. "This one here is Jackie Dooley. He lives just up the holler over yonder and this one is Dank. He's the one I stayed with last night."

"Don't you think you ought to tell them who I am?" Hambone's Grandfather chided.

"Oh, yeah." Hambone answered. "This is my Grandpappy. Folks call him Big Jim Mosely but I always call him Pappy."

Hambone's grandfather walked to Jackie and stuck out his hand. Jackie reached out his hand and it disappeared in the palm of Big Jim. He then reached his hand to me and I also reached out my hand. Big Jim's hand made my hand look like that of a newborn baby. His hand was calloused, and he gave me a firm but gentle handshake.

I heard the backdoor slam and saw Hambone's mother come walking back to the truck. Momma was standing in the door watching as Hambone's mother took Hambone by the hand and said, "Let's go, Honey. We got a lot of things to do before dark."

Hambone looked at me and said, "Thanks for letting me stay with you last night, Dank. Maybe you can spend a night with me pretty soon."

"That would be great!" I answered as I watched the three of them slide into the cab of the truck. Hambone's mother had slid to the middle of the seat and Hambone sat next to the passenger door. She placed her arm around his shoulder and hugged him close to her. Jackie and I watched as the truck pulled out of our driveway.

"That was a big man, Dank." Jackie said.

"Yep. He sure was." I replied.

"Do you still want to play some basketball?" Jackie asked.

"Sure." I answered as we walked toward the barn where the basketball goal hung above the door.

After taking a few steps I stopped and said, "Now I remember!"

"Remember what?" Jackie said.

"Now I remember where I saw Big Jim. It was at the wrestling match in Booneville last year. You remember when they brought a bunch of them wrestlers in and they wrestled in the gym at the High School?"

"No. I didn't get to go. My Grandma Ross was about to die then. That woman has been about to die for as long as I can remember. Daddy said she is going to be the death of him and that she'll outlive every one of her children. He called her an old hipo-kot-react or something like that." Jackie answered.

"Well, you sure missed something. They had a real live wrestling ring right in the middle of the basketball floor and they had midgets wrestle and women wrestle. When the two women came out and before they started to wrestle, Possum McIntosh climbed up into the ring. Daddy said he thought that Possum must have been two sheets in the wind. Anyway, Possum stood right in the middle of the ring and announced that whichever of them two women won the match would get him as a prize and she would become the next Mrs. Possum McIntosh. Both of them women and they were big women, grabbed Possum and pulled on him just like two dogs pulling on a dead rabbit and then slung him around just like he was a rag doll. They threw him back three rows into the crowd. The sheriff picked Possum up and I guess took him to jail. They even had the champion wrestler for the whole United States there that night. They had a fellow from Russia called the Russian Giant and he was a big old fellow. He came out into the ring and everyone booed him. Old Willie Spicer stood up, waved his cane at him and called him a Commie or I think that's what he called him. I didn't hear everything he said because momma cupped her hands over my ears.

Big Jim was there that night. They offered a hundred dollars to anyone in the crowd who could stay in the ring with a big old masked fellow they called the Black Cyclone for ten minutes. Big Jim crawled up under the ropes that were around the ring and stood up and beat his chest and shouted, "I'm just the man to beat that big old feller that's so ugly he has to wear a mask. Let's have a go at it!" There was a loud roar from the people in the gym and everybody was clapping their hands and stomping their feet. Little Mike Welch was sitting right in front of me and he got so excited he threw his bag of popcorn right up into the air and it landed all over me. Big Jim and that Black Cyclone eyed each other and started circling the ring. Then all of a sudden, that big old Black Cyclone run at Big Jim and Big Jim ran right at the Black Cyclone and they grabbed each other. Big Jim picked up the Black Cyclone just like he was a five-year-old boy, held him above his head and then walked over to the side of the ring and tossed him out onto the front row of people that were sitting there. Beat anything I ever saw in my whole life. Everybody just roared with laughter. I think the Cyclone must have broken his arm or ribs or something because he wouldn't climb back into the ring with Big Jim."

"I wish I could have seen that." Jackie said. Before we could begin our basketball game, I heard Momma yell at us from the house.

"Dank! Jackie's mother called. She wants him to come home right now!" She said emphasizing the word "Right." .

"Oh, Man!" Jackie said as he stomped his foot. "Guess I won't get a chance to show you some of my moves."

I smiled as Jackie turned and started to walk toward his home. Momma yelled again "She said for you to get home right now, Jackie."

I laughed as Jackie began to run.

"Dank, come on up to the house. I need to talk to you." Momma said.

I turned and walked slowly toward the house. As I did, I tried to think if I had done something wrong. I remembered doing my chores before Hambone and I had gone to the store that morning and she didn't seem to be upset with me at the dinner table. But, I reasoned, she might not have wanted to scold me in front of Jackie and Hambone. As hard as I thought, I couldn't think of anything that I might have done to make her upset with me.

When I walked into the kitchen I saw Momma sitting at the table. "Sit down here Dank." Momma commanded. "I've got some bad news to tell you." I obeyed and took a seat at the table.

"Hambone's daddy was killed this morning, Dank. That's where your Daddy is right now. I'm not sure how it happened, just that he was shot while working in his tobacco field at their old place."

"Who would have shot him?" I asked and then, "Why would anybody want to kill Hambone's daddy? He was a good man and a good daddy to Hambone."

"I don't know, Dank." Momma said as she wiped a tear from her eyes with a handkerchief. "You'll learn in life, Dank, that there are a lot of mean people in this world who don't value life very much... just interested, it seems, in their own selfish desires."

As I sat at the table, I tried to imagine how Hambone must be feeling. I tried to imagine how I would feel if I learned that my daddy had been shot dead.

The next few days were a whirlwind of activity. We attended the visitation and the funeral of Hambone's father. Momma and all the women in the community baked and cooked food, cleaned the house and did other household chores for the family during their time of grief. The men did all of the outside chores, cared for the livestock, plowed and hoed the garden, corn and tobacco crops.

It took a few weeks for everything to begin to settle back into a normal routine.

I had walked to the store to get some things for Momma. Pete Spivey and George Fry sat on the front porch of the store. They were engrossed in a game of checkers and didn't even acknowledge me when I stepped onto the porch and quietly took a seat near them. Upturned pop cases had been converted into makeshift chairs and they had stacked other pop cases on top of each other to make a table to hold their checkerboard. I stared at them, allowing my eyes to examine each of them from head to foot.

George was a short, fat man with a bulging stomach. He sat as near as he could to the checkerboard carefully examining the progress of the game. He wore a sweat stained felt hat, white dress shirt and faded dress pants.

Pete reminded me of a praying mantis. He was as tall and skinny as a bean pole. He wore a baseball cap, white t-shirt stained with ambeer juice, and wrinkled blue jeans. Pete was the only man I knew who could touch his knees with his hands without bending over. I watched as Pete leaned over the checkerboard moving his head in a circular motion, first going in a clockwise direction and then quickly reversing.

The only sound that disrupted the quietness of the early autumn morning was that of a crow circling a grove of maple trees on the opposite hillside and the clanging of checkers hitting the checker board. And then, George spoke.

"Pete, this old world is speedin' right on to a judgement day as sure as I'm a sittin' here.. It ain't going to last much longer. Every time I read the paper or listen to the news on the radio I know that this world is so out of whack that only the Good Lord can bring it back in shape. But I'm starting to think that He might just be of a notion to blow the whole thing up."

Pete only responded with a slow, "uuuuuum-huh" without removing his gaze from the checkerboard. After a few minutes of silence, Pete leaned back, stretched his arms and said, "God may not even have to do a thing about blowing it up, George. Seems like we're bound and determined on blowing ourselves up with them there 'tomic bombs. I wouldn't be surprised any day to wake up and find everything all around me blowed to smithereens."

Pete and George's discussion on the current state of world affairs was interrupted by Lying Andy Couch. He came to a screeching halt in his old green International Pick-up next to the gas pumps in front of the store. He quickly jumped out of the truck and began to put gas into his truck. As he stepped up onto the porch and entered the store to pay for his gas, he only muttered "howdy" seemingly as an afterthought. As he came back out of the store he stepped from the porch and headed toward his truck.

"Come on back here, Andy and tell us a big lie." George yelled.

Without even turning, Andy yelled back. "I ain't got time. Old man Zeke Moore died last night, and I got to get on over there and help get his poor old carcass ready to put into the ground." Andy sped away, leaving a cloud of dust and flying gravels in his wake.

Pete and George continued their game of checkers. "I shore hate to hear about old Zeke. He was a good old man. I allus saw him sitting in that old rocking chair on his front porch. He waved at everybody that went by." George said.

"Yep, but he lived a good long life. He had to be at least ninety." Pete answered.

"Recon we ought to go over to Zeke's? They may need us to help get the poor old man ready to bury." George suggested.

"Let's just leave the checkerboard and drive on over there." Pete said as he stood to his feet.

They then turned and saw me. "Why Dank, how long you been perched on that bench." Pete said.

"Quite a while." I answered.

"Well, we got us an errand of mercy to run. You have a good morning, Dank." Pete said as he and George stepped off the porch and walked to Pete's old gray Ford pickup. I watched as they pulled out of the store parking lot and turned toward Zeke's home.

I sat on the porch for a few minutes, then rose and walked into the store. Emma, the store owner, was behind the counter examining the customer books for those who were running a credit account. She looked up from her work and spoke, "Good morning Dank. Is your mom and dad doing well?"

"Yes Mam." I replied as I continued to the back of the store, opened the pop case and took out a RC Cola. I came back to the front of the store and sat down on the well-worn bench.

"Know any news?" Emma asked me as she continued to examine her customer accounts.

"Just heard that Zeke Moore died last night. Andy Couch, Pete and George were going over to his house to help get him ready for his coffin."

Emma looked up from her books and stared at me. "Well don't that beat all? I thought that old man was going to outlive everybody in this community. He's been an old man since the time I was a little girl. But, I guess it was just the Lord's time to take him on out of this world." She then turned her attention back to her work.

I heard a car pull up in front of the store and watched as Hank Rowlette entered. Hank was a coal miner and he was still covered in coal dust as he walked to the counter.

Emma raised up from the counter and spoke, "Good morning Hank. Looks like you're just getting off work."

"Yes Mam," Hank answered. Lula wanted me to stop on the way home and get a loaf of that light bread for my sandwiches this week. Could you get it for me and put it in a paper poke?"

"I sure can." Emma said. As she walked toward the bread display, she continued, "We just heard that old Zeke Moore died last night."

Hank looked at me and I could see the white around his brown eyes and his mouth was open, revealing two missing front teeth. "Then I just seen a ghost." He said.

As Emma walked back to the counter carrying a loaf of bread, she stopped momentarily, and then as in shock continued to the counter. "What do you mean?" Emma asked.

"I just came by Zeke's house and there he was, sitting in that old rocking chair and rocking like he was a little boy. He was waving at every car that went by and seemed to be enjoying it." Hank responded.

"Who told you that Zeke had died?" Emma asked me.

"Andy Couch." I answered.

"That old scoundrel!" Emma said. "He's done it again. I swear, you can't believe a word that man tells you. One day he's going to stand before the Good Lord and get his pay back for all those lies he's told. You just mark my words. I'm sure glad you told me about Zeke, Bill. I would have gone on blabbing that big old lie to everyone who came into this store if you hadn't stopped by"

Hank looked at me, smiled and then said, "Well. I better be getting on home. Lula will have something to eat waiting for me." He turned and left the store and I heard the engine of his truck start and the sound of it pulling away.

I sat in the store for a while longer and talked with Emma as she worked. I then stepped back out onto the porch and took my seat, slowly sipping on my RC Cola. While sitting there I saw Hambone coming up the road. There was no mistaking his red hair.

He came to the store, stepped up onto the porch, looked at me and smiled, slowly raising his right hand in a wave. Although he smiled, I saw that his eyes were sad. Without speaking to me, he entered the store.

While Hambone was in the store, I saw the old gray truck of Pete come flying back up the road and came to a screeching halt on the gravels of the store parking lot.

As Pete and George got out of the truck, I could see that they were mad. Their faces was red and their voices loud. They were using language describing Andy Couch that a small boy's ears should never hear. They came onto the porch, sat down at their makeshift checkerboard and resumed their game of checkers, continuing to describe everything they would do to Andy if he were there.

As Pete and Zeke were involved in their discussion, Hambone came out of the store and took a seat next to me. He was holding a Nehi grape pop in his hand and a Moon Pie. After a few moments of silence, I spoke.

"I ain't seen you in a while." I said.

"Nope." Hambone answered. "Mama wouldn't let me get off our place by myself. I swear, she is just like an old momma hen with her baby chicks." He took a bite of his Moon pie, a drink of his grape pop, and then continued. "They caught the old good for nothing heathen that shot my daddy."

"Who was it?" I asked.

His name is Joe York. He lived on the farm right next to our old place. Momma said that he was always jealous of Daddy because daddy took forty acres of scrub land and turned it into a good farm while he was always struggling to get any crop at all to grow on his farm."

"That don't seem much like a good reason to shoot and kill anyone." I said.

"Well, guess you have to know that old piece of cow dung to figure out that he don't have much sense of any kind at all. Daddy once said that Joe was always trying to blame everybody else for his own failures."

"What are they going to do to him?" I asked.

"Well, they got him locked up in the jail right now. I guess the trial will start pretty soon. It won't be any too soon for me. I hope they electrocute him and that I will get to watch it being done." Hambone said.

Our conversation was interrupted by the sound of Andy Couch's old green pickup coming to a stop in front of the store.

I whispered to Hambone, "Just watch this. This should be good."

Pete said to George, "Well look who is here, George. Just the man we been waiting to have some words with."

Andy got out of his truck and stepped onto the store porch. As he took the handle of the screen door without speaking, George yelled, "Andy Couch. You are about the nearest nothing to a man as any man I ever met. Who do you think you are to tell us that old man Zeke died last night? That old man is more alive than any of us here on this porch. Your big old lie caused me and Pete to make fools out of ourselves by running over there like bats out of the attic to help with his burial only to find him sitting on his front porch, rocking away, as big as life. We ought to whip you right now just like we would whip an old mangy dog."

Andy let go of the door handle and faced Pete and George. "Is that so?" Andy said, placing his hands on his hips and taking a defiant fighting stance. "Well, let me just ask you two fellers one question. When I stopped here earlier and you two was sitting right where you are right now, didn't you yell at me as I was going to my truck and tell me that you wanted me to come back up here and tell you a lie? Didn't you do that? Or have you fellers got a sudden loss of memory?"

George and Pete looked at each other as Andy continued, "I didn't need to take my precious time and interrupt my busy schedule to come all the way back up here onto the porch to give you fellers what you asked for. You asked me to tell you a lie and that's just what I did. Now if you don't really want something from a feller, then don't ever ask him for it. You might just get what you asked for!"

After finishing his speech, Andy went into the store while Pete and George continued to stare at each other. Pete started to giggle, and the giggle turned into a loud laugh. After a moment of seemingly stunned silence, George also started to laugh.

"Well, I gotta get home, Dank." Hambone said as he stood up. "Momma might worry if I stay away too long and I sure don't want to add any more worry to her than what she's already got."

I also stood and said, "I'll walk with you."

Hambone and I walked along the narrow gravel road in silence until Hambone finally spoke. "Pappy said the County Judge had turned Joe York over to the Grand Jury for killing my Daddy. They're meeting tomorrow and are going to do something about him, turn an "in-di-ment" or something another. Then I guess they'll have a trial.'

"When will the trial start?" I asked.

"Don't know." Hambone answered. "Maybe a week or two."

"I'm mad, Dank!" Hambone said. "Don't think I've ever been madder in my whole life. When I see the hurt in Momma's eyes and hear her cry, it makes me want to hurt Joe York real bad. It makes me want to cause him to suffer so much that he would beg for someone to kill him. He's a worthless piece of trash. He ain't even worth his weight in horse manure. My Daddy is twice the man that Joe York is."

Hambone paused, stopped and said, "I didn't say that right Dank. I guess I should have said that 'my Daddy WAS twice the man of Joe York."

"No, you said it right, Hambone." I answered as we began to walk again. "My Daddy said that I would always be his son and he would always be my Daddy. No matter what happened. Don't matter if I get put in jail or die or move all the way out of this country, Daddy said nothing would ever change the fact that we're blood kin and a hundred years from now people will still be saying that he was my Daddy and I was His son..... He said it's kinda like us and God. When we become a Christian then God becomes our Father and ain't nothing in Heaven or earth or hell that will ever change that."

"Hmmmm." Hambone said. "Hadn't thought of it that way Dank." And I saw the faint glimmer of a smile on Hambone's lips.

When I reached home, I said Goodbye to Hambone and ran up the small bank that led to the house. As I started into the side door, I turned to wave at Hambone, but he had already vanished. I felt a hurt deep down in my heart. I also knew what it felt like to lose someone that you love.

That night at supper Daddy told Momma about the events surrounding the trial of Joe York. "Joe York will be tried sometime next week." Daddy announced. "The Grand Jury will indict him tomorrow and Circuit Court is scheduled to start next Tuesday. He'll probably be the first case they try."

"What on earth would motivate him to shoot Wad Gabbard?" Momma asked.

"Well, from what I can gather," Daddy answered, "He claims that Wad was tending his tobacco crop on property that belonged to him. It wouldn't have been more than a ten foot stretch that they were disputing over. There had been bad blood between them for a good while."

"I can't believe that someone would kill another man over a little ten foot piece of property line." Momma said.

"Emma," Daddy answered, "I've known of men getting killed over six inches of property line. Don't you remember when Herman McIntire killed Breck Thomas? Herman had put up a stock fence around his property and the reason Breck gave for shooting him was because Herman had put the fence posts on property that Breck claimed belonged to him. Men do some strange things when it comes to their property lines."

On Wednesday of the following week we again sat at the supper table. Daddy mentioned to Momma that a jury had been selected and the trial of Joe York would begin the next day. Later in the meal Daddy said that he planned to attend the trial, then looking at me he said, "Would you like to go with me, Dank?" I looked up from my plate of beans, corn, mashed potatoes and chicken and with a mouth full of food answered, "I sure would."

That night I could hardly sleep. I had never attended a real to life murder trial before. I had been in the courtroom with Mikie Bishop whose Daddy was the county jailor. We had gone there to make sure the trash cans were emptied but I had never seen a true to life judge or jury or killer being tried.

After breakfast the next morning Daddy and I traveled to Booneville and entered the courthouse, climbing a set of stairs, to the courtroom. A large crowd of people were gathered in the hallway, slowly making their way into the large room. As each man entered the room, a deputy sheriff would search their pockets and run his hands over their waists, up and down their legs and ankles. They would have the women open their purses and one of the wives of the Deputies would do a similar search. When Daddy and I approached the door the deputy looked at Daddy, smiled and motioned us on into the room.

"Why didn't he search you, Daddy?" I asked.

"I'm Coroner." Daddy answered. I've got a right to carry my pistol anywhere at any time."

"Why didn't they search me?" I asked. "I'm not Coroner."

"No need to search boys your age. They just want to make sure that Wad's Daddy, or none of Wad's brothers, uncles or cousins try to end this trial before it even gets started." Daddy replied.

"How would they do that?" I asked.

"By shooting Joe dead," Daddy whispered as we took our seats.

I looked around the courtroom and saw men sitting at two tables. "Who are those men?" I asked Daddy.

"Those men over there are lawyers for Joe." Daddy said as he pointed to his left "and those men over there are what they call prosecutors. The tall man in the blue suit is the Commonwealth Attorney, Howard Ashcraft."

I saw Banford Bishop, Mikie's father escort Joe into the courtroom. He had chains on his feet and handcuffs on his wrists. He was a tall, skinny man with tousled hair. It looked like my hair in the morning when I had just gotten out of bed except it was red instead of black. He wore a faded plaid flannel shirt and overalls. He acted like a scared rabbit that had been cornered by a beagle hound, glancing nervously to his left and to his right.

I saw a group of people enter from the front of the courtroom and take seats to the right of the room. Daddy whispered in my ear, "That's the jury."

Soon the Circuit Judge, James Jackson, entered the courtroom and the High Sheriff, Clarence Treadway bellowed, "Everyone stand. Court is now in session with the Honorable James Jackson presiding." Everyone stood to their feet. After the Judge had taken his seat, everyone else sat down.

I looked at the face of the judge. He had a solemn expression on his face, his eyes piercing and his thin lips a narrow stretch of unmoving flesh until he spoke to the Sheriff, "Clarence, you can now read the indictment."

The High Sheriff rose to his feet and read from a piece of paper the charges against Joe. After he had finished the Judge commanded, "Will the defendant rise." Joe's attorneys nudged him and stood, half lifting Joe to his feet.

"How do you plead, guilty or not guilty?" The Judge asked. Joe looked at his attorneys and one of them spoke, "Not guilty Judge."

"All right," the Judge continued, "Then we'll begin to take care of the business at hand. Mr. Prosecutor, you can now begin to call your witnesses."

As the prosecutor called his witnesses, I gave my attention to the Jury. I knew four of them. One was Melvin Sebastian, a tall, lanky schoolteacher who lived on Cow Creek. Another was Daniel Horton, a store owner from Island Creek. He stuttered when he spoke, but he was known to be a good man. I saw Robert Robinson, a large man well over six feet tall and I could tell that he had a chew of tobacco in his mouth. He was holding tightly to a tin can in his right hand and would occasionally spit tobacco juice into it. The last one that I knew was

Doug Tirey, a short man with freckles and red hair. He was a livestock buyer and had made a good living for his family.

Following a flow of witnesses, the court was adjourned for lunch. As Daddy and I left the courtroom, Daddy said, "Dank, I'm going to take you back home. This will go on for the rest of the day and tomorrow. I need to finish a plumbing job over on Mistletoe."

I was disappointed but I meekly replied, "Okay."

At supper the following day, Daddy shared with Momma the outcome of the trial. I listened closely as he spoke:

"I guess everyone in the county is talking about the outcome of that trial, Emma. The court case ended about noon today. Banford took Joe back to the jail, guarded by some deputies. The Jury took off time for lunch at Campbell's Restaurant and then about one o'clock began to consider the evidence. By two o'clock they had reached a unanimous verdict of guilty and recommended Joe face death by electrocution."

"Well I can agree with that and I never even heard one word of the evidence." Momma replied. "From what I heard at the beauty shop last Friday morning, seems like it was an open and shut case."

"Well, there's one snag to the whole thing." Daddy announced. "Joe ain't never going to be electrocuted. For that matter, he ain't even going to spend one more day in jail."

Momma's mouth flew open as if she was a dying person gasping for air, "What!" She shouted. I looked at Momma and then at Daddy. Daddy took a bite of country ham, slowly chewed it, swallowed and then continued.

"Well, the Jury came back into the court room. Banford escorted Joe back to the court room and everybody else crammed into the room as well. When the Judge came into the room, he asked the Jury to give him their verdict. He asked Joe to stand and he did, with a little smile on his lips. The Judge looked at the verdict, handed it to Clarence and then Clarence read it out loud, "Guilty and death by electrocution."

Joe's face turned as white as a sheet and it was just like his knees gave out under him. His lawyers had to catch him and help him to sit down in his chair.

Then it happened. Storm Gabbard, Wad's brother was sitting right behind Joe. I still can't figure that out. To me that would have been a dead giveaway as to what was going to happen next."

Daddy took another bite of food and began to slowly chew. Momma was sitting motionless, watching Daddy slowly chew and finally she said. "Bob…. Hurry up and swallow that food right now. You're not an old bossy cow that has to chew their wad all day. Tell me what happened."

Daddy swallowed his food as ordered and continued. "When Joe sank down into his seat, Storm took out a 38-caliber snub-nosed pistol and shot him twice right in the back of the head. Killed him right on the spot. Everything was pure pandemonium. Women were screaming, men were shouting, children were crying. Storm dropped his gun to the floor and then held his hands straight up into the air. The Judge came out from behind the bench with a pistol in his hand and then ordered Clarence to take Storm into custody and to clear the courtroom. They took Storm to jail."

"How did he get the pistol, Daddy?" I asked. "When you and me were there yesterday the deputies were searching everybody."

Daddy looked at me and said, "Your friend Hambone, Dank. They weren't searching the children…. Just the grownups. Hambone had slipped the gun into the courtroom and passed it to Storm."

"Did they put Hambone in jail?" I asked.

"No. Sent him home with his Momma." Daddy answered.

That night as I lay in bed I thought about Hambone and Storm. I thought about Storm shooting Joe York in the back of the head and questioned what I would do if anyone had killed one of my family? Would it make me so angry that I would seek vengeance against the killer? I thought about Hambone slipping the gun into the courtroom. If someone had killed my father would I also want to have a part in that vengeance, however small?

The next day I walked to the store and took a seat on the front porch. Three of the old men were talking about the events of the day before and the excitement it had caused within the county.

Daniel Dooley said, "Well, I think when it comes right down to it, the Jury found that man guilty as sin and that boy – what's his name – Storm? Anyway, he saved the state a lot of money by just doing the executioner's job."

"I guess you could say that." Pete Spivey agreed. "But what if'n he wanted to appeal that verdict. Seems like that is what all them guilty people do anymore. Can't ever tell, but he might have found a court somewhere that would have determined he was as innocent as a newborn baby."

George Fry cleared his throat and said, "I ain't worried none about that murdering devil. I'm just worried about what might happen to that feller that took his brother's killing to heart and did exactly what anyone of us sitting here would have done if we had been thrown into the same place."

They continued to talk back and forth for a while, and I saw Hambone walking slowly up the road toward the store. He stepped up onto the porch and sat down next to me. The men stopped talking about the events surrounding the trial and changed the topic to their tobacco crops.

"I need to talk to you, Dank." Hambone said, "Can we walk around to the side of the store?"

"Sure" I said as I stood and the two of us walked to the side of the building.

Hambone looked at his feet and said, "We're going to be moving, Dank. Momma says that we're selling everything and going to move up north. Probably Ohio. She's afraid that the York family will try to do something to me or to her. Storm is probably going to have to leave the county too." Hambone lifted his head and I saw tears in his eyes.

"I don't want to move, Dank. But I guess we're going to have to and Momma is going to need me to help her."

"I understand." I said. "I hate to see you leave Hambone. You've been a good friend and I'll miss you a lot."

Hambone smiled, wiped the tears off his cheeks with the back of his hand and then reached out his hand to shake mine.

After we shook hands, Hambone said. "They let Storm out of jail. Judge didn't even set no bond for him and the Commonwealth

Attorney has told Storm that he don't plan to bring no charges against him. Said they wouldn't be able to find twelve men in the whole county that would find him guilty anyways. He's going up to Dayton and get a job, I guess."

"I'm glad." I said. "Will I see you again, Hambone?" I asked.

"Sure." He answered. "We'll come back sometimes. I'll try to let you know when we do and maybe we can go fishing."

I smiled. "That will be good." I said.

"Well, I gotta get back home. I just wanted to see you before we left and your Momma told me you were here."

I nodded as Hambone turned and started to walk back down the road. As he did, I couldn't help but wonder if I would ever see him again.

I slowly walked back to the porch of the store and took a seat. The men once again turned their topic of conversation to the trial and killings, but their words were blurred by the thoughts and memories that raced through my own mind and I began to hum the tune to Hambone and mumbled to myself a new verse that came to my mind:

Hambone, hambone when you comin' back?
Won't be long Dank, you can bank on that
and I'll be drivin' a long cadillac
Hambone

Chapter 8

Snakes and Baptisms

Aunt Lovely Biggs was the ugliest woman I had ever seen. She was tall, gangly, and thin faced and her hair reminded me of a ragged mop that had seen much better days and was on the verge of being discarded. Of course, I was only seven years old and I had not seen everyone in the world, but my opinion of Aunt Lovely was also held by my father. He was much older than me and had travelled to places I had never seen. He had seen far more people than I had seen, and I overheard him tell my mother one Sunday on our traditional ride to our Grandmothers following church. "Here we are on our way to your mother's home from church, Emma and I'm trying to figure out something that the preacher said this morning."

"I thought it was a good sermon, Bob. He preached a whole sermon on that verse from Ecclesiastes about all things being beautiful. I thought he did a really good job at describing all the beauty of the world and people around us. What are you wondering about?"

Well, the preacher did say, and he read it right out of the Bible, mind you, that 'He made everything beautiful in His time.' When he read that I couldn't help but look at Lovely Biggs and Emma, I swear that woman is as ugly as sin. I've heard people always use the term, 'ugly as mud" and I don't know how ugly mud is supposed to be but I do know that mud don't have any leg up on Lovely Biggs."

"Bob!" momma responded. "You ought to be ashamed of yourself.

I do agree that Lovely isn't quite as pretty as most people but she is beautiful inside."

"Maybe so." Daddy answered. "Problem is we can't turn her inside out to see what she looks like inside."

"Now that's not true, Bob." Momma chided. "Whenever she sings it's as beautiful a sound as any songbird God ever created could make. That comes from inside….. Right straight from her heart."

There was silence for a few minutes and Daddy spoke again.

"Maybe old Will Frost had a premonition about Lovely when she was born. Maybe he knew that his only child was going to be as ugly as cairn and he hoped that by giving her a lovely name it would make it less painful for her and everyone else that would have to look at her. Some of the men say that after Will and Lida saw how ugly she was as a baby, they just didn't have any desire to have any more young'uns."

"We need to talk about this later, Bob." Momma said. "You've got some little ears listening to everything that you're saying."

There was silence for a moment and then I heard Daddy mumble, "I don't know what those little ears have heard but I can tell you that it can't compare to what those little eyes see every time they look at Lovely Biggs."

I saw Momma shake her head back and forth and then she turned her eyes to the window of the car as though she was looking at the homes and familiar landscape that we sped by.

We reached the turn from the main road onto the winding dirt and gravel road that would take us to Grandma's house at the head of the long hollow. After we made the turn, Momma turned and looked at me, saying, "Now Dank, when we get there I don't want you running off with Ronnie and Donnie (my cousins) into the woods and getting your clothes all dirty and messing them up. I want you to sit down on the porch and don't you move until after we eat dinner and start to the Baptizing this afternoon."

"Awwwww Momma, I won't get dirty." I whined.

"You heard me, Dank." She responded. "You just try getting off that porch and you know what will be in store for you, young man."

I knew well what Momma was talking about. Her favorite device for punishment was a quarter inch thick yard stick from Barrett's Hardware. I think that the hardware store must have ordered a case of them just for Momma each year because she always seemed to break them across my backside, causing her to become even angrier with me. I hadn't seen her place the yardstick into the car but I also knew that my Aunts always kept a good supply on hand and that Momma could borrow one from them.

Through the years I had also discovered an important fact. When I had been much younger, I would always try to run from Momma as she prepared to render her motherly punishment. She would hold my hand with her left hand and then, with her right hand make a large sweeping swing, much like I had seen Daddy do with his mowing scythe. The force of the yardstick would sting my backside. Either by chance or perhaps it was an attempt to gain mercy, on one of my mother's administrations of judgement, I had latched onto her leg and discovered that she was unable to make a large sweeping swing with the yardstick, but instead, had to settle for a shorter swipe. I knew nothing about physics or the law of motion and force, but I did know I had made a discovery that at least for my purposes, would rival that of Columbus.

When we arrived at the large, sprawling white frame house of my Grandmother, I saw my Aunts, Uncles and Cousins gathered on the porch. I quickly jumped out of the back seat and raced to the porch to join them while Momma and Daddy retrieved a cake, pie and large bowl of potato salad from the trunk.

Ronnie and Donnie, my cousins, were sitting on the edge of the porch, their legs dangling over the side. I sat next to them. We sat silent for a few minutes until Donnie asked, "You going to the baptizing?" I nodded my head yes.

A few more minutes of silence passed, and Donnie spoke again, "You been baptized Dank?"

"No." I responded. "Have you?"

"No, I don't think so. At least not by a Preacher but, maybe I have, though. Ronnie and me were down at the swimming hole one day when I was five years old and Ronnie told me that I needed to be baptized or I would go to Hell for sure. I didn't want to go to Hell so I started to cry and asked Ronnie what I could do. He said that he could baptize me right then and there so he doused me under the water and said something I couldn't hear. He held me under for a long time and I thought I was going to drown for sure but he baptized me. Do you recon that would count for being baptized?"

"I don't think so." I responded. "I think you have to be baptized by an honest to goodness preacher for it to count for anything."

I saw a look of fear on Donnie's face as he whispered, "Does that mean I'm going to Hell?" I shrugged my shoulders and then looked at Ronnie who winked at me and smiled.

After we ate dinner all the family loaded into their cars and trucks to make the six-mile trip to a spot on Buck Creek where baptisms were usually held. There was ample parking at the side of the road and a large hole of water with a level bank that was a perfect location for such an event.

When we arrived at the location, several cars had already parked near the Creek and people were gathered by the side of the gently flowing stream. As we walked to the creek Momma whispered to me, "Now Dank, You better be on your best behavior. This is a very solemn occasion and no time for you to be acting up. Do you hear me, young man?" she asked

"Yes Momma." I responded.

After taking our place at the side of the creek, Donnie came and stood next to me. Together we walked to the fringe of the large crowd that was gathering and took a seat on the rocky bank of the creek.

"Wish I had brought my fishing pole." Donnie said. "Me too." I agreed.

Preacher Pendergrass walked to the edge of the creek and very carefully moved out into the clear water of the stream. Soon he was standing waist deep in the water, holding in his right hand a clean white handkerchief. He was a large man with a balding head and a long gray mustache. He wore a white shirt and black pants and as he raised his right hand into the air, his booming voice said, "Amen…. Amen…. We're going to get started here!" Everyone became quiet.

"All right people. We're glad you're here. Today we are going to witness the gloooooooorious fruits of an outpouring of Goooooooooods grace as we baaaaaaaaaptize three precious souls. But first, we're going to sing a hymn and Brother Willie Margraves is going to lead us." I was amazed at the ease with which Preacher Pendergrass could cause words to become sentences in themselves along with his ability to choose which word should be given that honor.

Willie Margraves took a place in front of the crowd and said, "We're going to sing a song that everyone here knows. We're going to sing, *Shall We Gather at the River*. So everyone, let your voices be heard and sing it out loud and strong." A hundred or more voices began to sing,

Shall we gather at the river,
Where bright angel feet have trod,
With its crystal tide forever
Flowing by the throne of God?
Yes, we'll gather at the river,
The beautiful, the beautiful river;
Gather with the saints at the river
That flows by the throne of God.

As the crowd began to sing, I turned to see little Bruce Becknell standing behind us. Bruce was in my grade at Needmore School. He was dressed in his Sunday clothes and he motioned for me to come to where he was standing. I nudged Donnie and together we walked over to Bruce and he said, "Follow me." We followed Bruce a few yards up the creek and into a small grove of young water maples.

Bruce said, "I want to show you something." He reached into his pockets and pulled out two rubber snakes. One of them was about two feet long and the other about half the size." What do you think?" He asked.

"Those look like the real thing." Donnie said.

"Where did you get them?" I asked.

"Ralph Becknell had them and I traded him seven cats' eye marbles and a Superman comic book I'd read a hundred times for them." Bruce answered.

"You recon they would float on water." I asked.

"Sure they would!" Bruce declared.

"No, I don't think they would." Donnie said. "They're way too heavy."

"They're not that heavy and I know they will float." Bruce insisted.

"I don't know Bruce." I said as I took one of the snakes into my hand and moved it up and down several times. "They do feel awful heavy to me. I have to agree with Donnie. I don't think they will float on water."

"No, they are not too heavy!" Bruce almost screamed. "I'll prove it to you." He walked to the edge of the gently flowing creek and tossed them both into the water.

Bruce proved his point and the two rubber snakes floated on top of the water, just like real snakes.

I glanced down the creek as the last verse of the hymn was being sung. Gertie Miller had waded out to where the preacher stood and would have the honor of being the first of the three to be baptized that afternoon. Gertie was a large, matronly woman with slightly graying hair. Some folks said she had been a bootlegger during her earlier years. No one seemed to hold any ill will toward her for having that occupation. Her husband had been killed while working in the logging woods, and it seems that most folks reasoned that she was just trying to provide for her family and that she could ply her trade at home while keeping watch over her four little ones.

I turned to see Bruce at the edge of the creek as he was trying to fish his two rubber snakes out of the water. He lost his footing, slipped and sat down in the water causing a ripple that took the snakes out into the middle of the stream. I watched as they floated side by side down the creek toward Preacher Pendergrass and Gertie.

At the last word of the hymn, Preacher Pendergrass turned Gertie so that she was facing up the creek. He raised his hand into the air and said, "We praise God for the gloooooorisous salvation of Sister Gertie Miller, And now Lord we baaaaaaaaptize her into the fellowship of the

New Hope Baptist Church." He placed the clean white handkerchief over the nose and mouth of Gertie and started to lean her back into the clear water of the creek.

Suddenly Gertie, with eyes opened wide in fright, took Preacher Pendergrass' hand and fought his efforts to lower her backwards into the creek. She struggled to keep her footing, attempting to scream but unable to do so with the handkerchief over her mouth. After a struggle, she freed herself from the grip of the Preacher. Gertie pointed up the creek and began to scream, "Water Moccasins!! Water Moccasins!! Lord have mercy on us. We're being attacked by a horde of Water Moccasins coming down the creek."

I watched as Gertie, now freed from the grip of the preacher, struggled to make it to the bank of the creek. In the process of freeing herself from the firm grip of Preacher Pendergrass, she had managed to cause the preacher to lose his footing and he had fallen backwards into the water, immersing himself in a self-act of baptism. The other two candidate's for baptism had already reached dry land. Two of the men stepped into the water to assist Gertie in her flight to safety while Ted Houndshell, with his pistol drawn, rushed to the aid of Preacher Pendergrass.

"We better get back to the others." I suggested. Bruce and Donnie agreed and together we slipped quietly back into the crowd.

When Gertie reached dry ground some of the women came to her aid, handing her a towel and patting her gently on the back. Preacher Pendergrass regained his footing and guarded closely by Ted Houndshell, the two men joined Gertie on the bank of the creek. I watched the two rubber snakes float gently down the stream.

There was clear pandemonium among the crowd. Eyes turned up the creek looking for other snakes to appear while others watched the offending serpents disappear in the distance. A few within the crowd stared at each other in disbelief of what they had just witnessed.

Preacher Pendergrass regained his composure and said, "Brothers and Sisters…. Please Brothers and Sisters let me have your attention." The crowd grew quiet and Preacher Pendergrass continued. "Once again that old serpent, the devil, has attempted to bring confusion to the people of God! But I am here to tell you that he ain't going to stop this baptizing from happening today. While some of the men go up the creek and check for any other of them minions of Satan, I'm going to ask Sister Lovely Biggs to come up here and sing a special song for us. Be quiet now while Sister Lovely sings."

Several of the men, with pistols in their hands, strolled up the creek examining the water and the water maple grove that we had just vacated.

I watched Lovely Biggs slip through the crowd and take her place next to the preacher. She showed a shy demeanor of unworthiness to perform such an holy act but then, clearing her voice, she began to sing, As I went down to the river to pray, Studying about that good ol' way, And who shall wear the starry crown?, Good Lord show me the way! O sisters let's go down, Let's go down, come on down, O sisters let's go down, Down to the river to pray."

I watched as the women began to smile and sway to the lyrics of the hymn while the men stared at their feet or looked in any direction other than at the face of Aunt Lovely. Aunt Lovely didn't seem to notice the reaction of either the men or women, perhaps because she had her eyes closed and her face turned upward toward the clear sky as she loudly sang, "As I went down to the river to pray, Studying about that good ol' way, And who shall wear the robe and crown? Good Lord show me the way. O brothers let's go down, let's go down, come on down Come on brothers, let's go down, Down to the river to pray."

After Aunt Lovely completed her special song there were choruses of "Amen" and "Yes, Lord" by the assembly. Aunt Lovely smiled, lowered her head in polite modesty, and returned to the front of the crowd.

Preacher Pendergrass stepped forward and announced, "All right, Brothers and Sisters, we're going to complete the Lord's work in this place today. I want some of you men to go out into the creek with us and form a wall of protection against any more of Satan's demon snakes that might try to keep us from baptizing these precious souls into the fellowship of the church. And I want the rest of you to be watching and praying."

Several of the men stepped forward, slipped off their shoes, and stepped into the creek, obediently following the instructions of Preacher Pendergrass. The Preacher stepped into the creek for a second time and facing the crowd said, "All right Sister Gertie, let's try this again." Gertie cautiously followed the Preacher into the water, all the while, her eyes wide open and her head turning in all directions to survey the creek for any other threats to her safety.

The remainder of the baptismal service went without interruption. Our return trip home was quiet except for a brief conversation I overheard between my mother and father.

Daddy had started to laugh, and momma had said, "What are you laughing about, Bob?"

"Oh, just about the baptizing." He answered and then continued, "But I have to admit that I got to give old Preacher Pendergrass a lot of credit. He sure is one smart man."

Momma looked at daddy and said, "Just this morning you were questioning what he preached in church. What has caused you to change your mind about him?"

Daddy answered, "Well, he was smart enough to figure out that if there were any more snakes around, once they got a gander at Lovely Biggs, they would all slither right back into the deepest part of the woods they could find."

I saw Momma shake her head and heard her sigh as daddy continued to laugh.

That evening at supper Daddy said, "Dank, after we eat I need your help in the barn with a little chore.

After we finished supper, I followed Daddy to the barn and as we entered the large doors, I caught the familiar smell of fresh hay and livestock manure. We walked about half way into the building when Daddy stopped and turned to face me. Getting down on his knees and staring into my face, he said, "Dank, I don't really have anything for you to do, son, but I need to ask you a question and I didn't want to say anything in front of your Momma. Today at the baptizing I saw you, Donnie and the Becknell boy disappear into the woods above the creek and then suddenly, as all the commotion was taking place, you reappeared. You don't happen to know anything about what happened, do you?"

I looked into Daddy's large brown eyes, nodded my head "yes" and then shared with him what had happened.

Daddy stood, patted me on the head and then said, "Well, Dank. This don't ever need to be mentioned again to anyone. I guess you probably learned a lesson today, didn't you? And in case you don't know what that lesson is, I'm going to tell you. Can you imagine what would have happened the day that Ole John the Baptist was baptizing the Lord Jesus and you boys had been there pulling those rubber snake shenanigans? I can't hardly imagine what the Bible would read like today if that baptizing had been broken up like the baptizing today was. Always remember, Dank, snakes and baptisms just don't go very well together."

The Boy Within

I climbed the mountain with feeble step-
A walking cane my only help
And when I reached the mountain's crest
I paused a while for needed rest.
I took a seat on a fallen tree
as dimming eyes strained to see
what changes time must have made
to this place where I had played
as a boy - shirtless – carefree
beneath the arms of these friendly trees.
Familiar sounds came to my ears
that I had heard in long past years-
A chatting squirrel and the caw of crow
that warned of a stranger down below.
Before me lay a winding ridge
that turned into an earthen bridge
and carried me into the past
before my lot in life was cast.
With eye of mind I clearly traced
the path on which a small boy raced
with shoeless feet on leaf clad soil.
He raced for pleasure and not in toil.
He had no place that he must go
as he answered squirrel and caw of crow.
He was not shackled by fleeting time,

nor poets need to find a rhyme.
His mind was free to dream great things,
to mimic the song that crickets sing
and run his race with summers breeze
atop this mountain – beneath these trees.
A smile adorned my aging face
as a question formed and took a place
within my mind already filled
by a lifetime of days and thoughts concealed,
of dreams still dreamed, of work undone
of days of shadow and days of sun.
Where is this boy my mind's eye sees;
who ran his race with summers breeze;
whose mind was free to dream great things
and mimic the song the cricket sings?
As I stood from my needed rest
and turned to leave the mountains crest
the answer to my question came
refreshing as the summer's rain
The boy yet lives in a clever disguise
of an ageing man with dimming eyes;
who climbs mountains with feeble step –
A walking cane his only help.

CPSIA information can be obtained
at www.ICGtesting.com
Printed in the USA
FSHW022140281019